SHADI GHADIRIAN

Iranian Photographer

ISBN: 978-0-86356-638-7

Copyright © Shadi Ghadirian, 2008
Text ©   Rose Issa, 2008, unless otherwise indicated
Foreword © Marta Weiss, 2008
Editing: Katia Hadidian
Design: Normal Industries

This first edition published in 2008

A full CIP record for this book is available from the British Library.
A full CIP record for this book is available from the Library of Congress.

Manufactured in Lebanon by Chemaly & Chemaly

SAQI

26 Westbourne Grove, London W2 5RH
825 Page Street, Suite 203, Berkeley, California 94710
Tabet Building, Mneimneh Street, Hamra, Beirut
www.saqibooks.com

SHADI GHADIRIAN

Iranian Photographer

Edited by Rose Issa

SAQI

London San Francisco Beirut

Beyond Art
PRODUCTIONS

FOREWORD

Shadi Ghadirian works in layers. In the five series of photographs included in this book, women's bodies are by turn obscured by layers of fabric, hidden behind household objects, obliterated by crude strokes of black marker, concealed behind smudged windows, or swallowed by a screen of black pixels. These physical layers represent the more figurative – and often contradictory – layers of meaning that also overlap one another in Ghadirian's work. The women in her photographs are sandwiched between tradition and modernity, past and present, East and West, public and private, reproductions and originals, and reality and fantasy.

The layering effect is at its most complex in the first project presented here, the *Qajar Series*. The photographs in this series are re-creations of studio portraits made in Iran during the Qajar period, which spanned the second half of the nineteenth century to the first two decades of the twentieth. Several of the sitters are dressed in approximations of Qajar fashion, with short, full skirts over loose trousers and heavy, unplucked eyebrows. Others are completely veiled. Printed in the warm grey tones of nineteenth-century photographs, they feature all the typical accoutrements of studio portraiture of that period: a carpeted floor, carved wooden chair, painted backdrop, and sitters in stiff, stylised poses. In keeping with the practice of many such studio portraits, Ghadirian's also include props meant to reveal something of the identity – or aspirations – of the sitter. It is here that Ghadirian's version of the studio portrait breaks with the past, however, for her sitters pose with props such as a mountain bike, vacuum cleaner or can of Pepsi.

The jarring contrast of these modern consumer goods with the old-fashioned style of the portraits is indicative of the tensions between tradition and modernity and between public personas and private desires that many Iranian women navigate on a daily basis. The incongruity of the props also makes plain the artifice and theatricality of the studio portrait more generally. The women take on prescribed poses for the camera,

sitting or standing in front of scenery that is nothing
more than a flat layer of canvas, painted to resemble
the three-dimensional setting of a bucolic landscape
or a room decorated with an ornate mantelpiece and
plush, tasselled curtains.

What is perhaps even more surprising than the
incongruously modern props in the *Qajar Series*
photographs are the original images on which they
are based, which are themselves heavily layered
with seemingly contradictory motifs. The actual
Qajar portraits feature women in clothing that is
more revealing than what Iranian women are now
allowed to wear in public, and also contain modern
props, such as clocks or even bicycles, which are
indicative of the cosmopolitanism and comparative
liberalism of Iran during the Qajar period. What is
truly jarring about Ghadirian's re-stagings of century-
old photographs is that the clash between tradition
and modernity appears greater today than it might
have seemed a hundred years ago.

Ghadirian draws upon photographic styles and
processes that span the history of photography,
from nineteenth-century studio portraiture to digital
imagery manipulated, viewed and disseminated
by computer. The five bodies of work included
here are aesthetically distinct, but in all of them,
Ghadirian addresses the multi-layered experience
of contemporary Iranian women.

Marta Weiss
Curator, Photographs
Victoria and Albert Museum, London

'I am a photographer,
and this is the only thing I know how to do'

'I deal with social issues that concern me and inspire me. In the Domestic series, a woman is condemned to repetitive routines of tea making, preparing meals, cleaning, sweeping and serving. In Iran, few people live on their own, especially girls. The only time we are faced with practical domestic duties is when we are married, hence the association of domestic chores with marriage. Had I lived alone for some time, like many of my friends in Europe, maybe such work would not have inspired me' Shadi Ghadirian

LIKE THIS

Shadi Ghadirian's photographs are startling. They transcend geographical boundaries to bring us into direct contact with another world.

Ghadirian is one of the most outstanding young photographers of her generation, born in Tehran in 1974, at the height of the Iranian economic and cultural boom and just a few years before the Islamic Revolution. She came to the limelight in the late 1990s with her *Untitled* Qajar series, and since then has become one of the most active and inspiring artists from Iran – one who exhibits widely in Europe, the United States, the Middle East and beyond, and is collected by museums worldwide. Her fascination with the paradoxical life of women in Iran today, which takes place mostly behind closed doors, is a spirited wink at authority and shows the witty parody of social expectations, social restrictions and loopholes that form her life and times.

Ghadirian's own life and work is shaped by the rules and restrictions of post-revolutionary Iran, a rich source of subject matter. In the past thirty years, Iran has experienced far-reaching change in politics, society and the arts. Artists there face censorship, import-export restrictions, the absence of a cultural infrastructure to promote art, poor supplies and equipment[1] and few professional galleries[2]; most recently, global banking sanctions force Iranian artists and galleries to rely on complicated financial transactions to receive payment for their work. In spite of this, the country keeps producing artists of the highest calibre.

Photography has always had a strong following in Iran, ever since the Qajar court enthusiastically embraced it in the mid-nineteenth century, when Nasser el-Din Shah (1831–96) became a keen photographer and prolific collector of photographs. After the Islamic revolution of 1979, there was an intense focus on photography once again as Iranians rushed to document their surroundings during the long and destructive Iran-Iraq war (1980–8).

Photographers followed in the wake of Iran's internationally successful new-wave film-makers, and the visits of many Iranian artists in exile who came back to Iran for inspiration, such as Shirin

Neshat and Shirana Shahbazi. Moreover, the Middle East, and in this case Iran, with all its complex and intricate social histories, is simply a rich and aesthetically inspiring place: artists do not need to invent a pure concept in order to work. There is already much to say: the raw material, unexplored aesthetics and life stories are all there.

Furthermore, it is a good time to be a photographer in Iran. When Ghadirian graduated in 1998 from Azad University, she was one of the first to graduate from the photography department. Tehran had a few modest art galleries, and of those, only a handful accepted photography as an art form. The art scene has changed immensely in the last few years. Interest in photography has exploded and galleries are now competing with each other, sometime hiring large hotel halls to exhibit their artists. Photographers, who used to work mainly for newspapers and magazines (which were censored and gradually closed down), have finally started making a decent living from their work. Galleries are hunting young talent, collectors are buying sometimes haphazardly priced works, but the buzz is there and the market is encouraging young talent to come out.

Ghadirian's work is almost exclusively about the personal concerns of Iranian women of her generation. The evolution of her work over the last decade has its own social context: she illustrates the quest of teenage youth for more liberty, questions women's assigned roles and endless domestic chores, explores the quest for a more colourful life, reveals the reach of censorship, and wonders about the fate of a generation living in front of a computer. Ghadirian's work is therefore autobiographical, a visual contact with the country and its systems. Above all, hers is a perfect example of how photography can have a social function and maintain the highest visual and technical aesthetics.

UNTITLED QAJAR SERIES, 1998–1999

Before and after her graduation, Ghadirian worked as a part-time assistant to her teacher, the photographer and photography historian Bahman Jalali, who founded Iran's Photography Museum[3] with his wife Rana Javadi. At the time, Jalali and Javadi were the most enthusiastic photographers and publishers in

Iran, and it was with the encouragement of Jalali that Ghadirian became interested in Qajar king Nasser el-Din Shah's vast archive of nineteenth-century photographs – some 20,000 albums that are still intact at the Golestan Museum in Tehran.

Ghadirian started work on some thirty photographs for her graduation project. She studied the images and poses of Qajar women from the time when photography was first introduced in Iran in 1844. She recreated her own formal studio portraits, in black and white, with specially made or borrowed Qajar backdrops and costumes. She persuaded her sisters, friends and neighbours to sit for pictures, and scrupulously choreographed the formal poses of the Qajar women. She then introduced objects from her daily life: a CD player, television, vacuum cleaner, Pepsi can, bicycle, helmet, guitar, painting, a mirror reflecting censored books, beer cans and the *Hamshahri* newspaper, where she also worked (which was repeatedly banned and re-opened). These objects are 'forbidden', yet slip through customs into the black market and people's homes, while others are restricted – only women are forbidden to ride bicycles.[4]

When no forbidden objects are in sight, Ghadirian's women are completely veiled, resembling beautiful, abstract forms as decorative and inanimate as an empty flowerpot. Others look at you with a serene but forceful gaze, their veil lifted, which in Qajar times symbolised protest. These simple gestures hide complex codes and rules, and the overall effect is playful, light and elegant. The anachronisms highlight the loopholes, the many ways 'imported' products – films, videos, books, magazines, drinks – can infiltrate a culture, even if everything looks traditional to the outside observer.

Following her first solo exhibition at Lili Golestan's gallery in Tehran, Ghadirian was invited to exhibit this series at the Guildhall University in London in 1999, and her trip was sponsored by The Tehran Museum of Contemporary Art (they seem to have regretted this later). However, Ghadirian was surprised by Londoners' reaction to her work: they thought that this was how women in today's Iran actually dressed, and misread her work, failing to see its wit and to understand the duality and contradictions of life for young women in Iran. Ghadirian's objective was to display the contradictions and paradoxes of her society, to present women who cannot be defined by the period to which they belong. Her defiant and haughty subjects enact the schizophrenic life that they are obliged to lead, and the images hint that a healthy spirit of defiance is alive and well in Iranian homes.

Two years after her graduation, Ghadirian married Payman Houshmandzadeh, a writer and photographer known for his images of urban working-class men, captured in the hustle and bustle of Tehran's streets – the opposite of Ghadirian's approach. Upon her marriage, she left her family home for the first time, as few young women in Iran live on their own unless they are from a privileged background, and even then, it is not socially acceptable. Suddenly Ghadirian had to face the daily chores of domestic life; she had to cook, iron and clean for the first time. She had to be a housekeeper as well as a photographer and wife. (Like many women who want their children to study and succeed, Ghadirian's mother spared her domestic duties at home.) Ghadirian was also perplexed by the many wedding presents she received that were to do with housekeeping. This new life inspired her second, well-known series, *Like Every Day,* which explores the expectations made of married women in traditional societies, sentenced to a lifetime of cleaning, ironing and preparing food for their family.

In this series Ghadirian does not use the black chador that is seen in so many pictures of Iran, but rather the richly patterned, colourful, feminine and soft chadors that women traditionally wear inside their homes to receive guests. Ghadirian juxtaposes her faceless subjects wearing these 'home' chadors with domestic equipment: an iron, a broom, a kettle, a tea cup, pots and pans, dish-washing gloves and tools. This series of photographs then led to a commission by *Bidoun* magazine about domesticity in the Arab world, where housework is carried out mostly by maids from the Far East and South Asia – the new slaves of the Gulf.

With this series, Ghadirian began to be openly criticised by some Iranian public institutions, which found the work too critical of women's traditional roles. Rather than directly confronting her critics, once again she used reality and humour to visualise restrictions, including censorship.

CENSORS' SERIES, 2003-04

Having encountered a great deal of success and attention outside Iran, Ghadirian was invited to travel to attend her international exhibition openings. During these travels she started to read books and magazines that are not available in Iran, in particular publications promoting art and artists. She became aware of the gulf between this visual culture and what can be seen, read or shown in Iran, where art history books are censored, nude paintings deleted, pages with religious or sexual scenes ripped out, and fashion magazines almost entirely stamped in black ink to cover any exposed arms, legs or other body parts. This was to inspire another series of studio portraits in which she asked friends to wear their everyday clothes – the ones under their obligatory cover-ups – and to pose like the models in foreign magazines. Ghadirian then blackened everything that should not be shown officially in public, resulting in another witty exploration of private life, public life and fashion. She reveals the daily paradoxes of young women of her generation, the schizophrenia of dressing for outside and inside the home, of desiring fashion and change while having to follow strict and archaic social rules.

BE COLOURFUL SERIES, 2004-05

The interest in fashion and a flirtation with another, more colourful life hidden behind grey, beige or black chadors and veils, developed into another project: *Be Colourful*. Here Ghadirian played with friends and models in her studio, asking them to wear their favourite colours – orange, blue or red – and then photographed them through glass painted with a thin layer of grey paint. The resulting images appear as if we are looking through an outdoor window at an interior scene, from a public place into a private domain. The viewer peeps through the glass to see what women really want, what they consider appealing: more colour, nuance and variety in daily life.

CTRL+ALT+DEL SERIES, 2006-07

During my many visits to Iran in the last ten years, I have often discussed with artists the desperate need for more publications to make their work better known to the wider public. There is a conspicuous absence of information about artists living in Iran. When I applied in Europe for funding to publish monographs or thematic works on artists from a country with endless emerging talents, but very isolated politically, I encountered several difficulties: funding bodies preferred to give money to the countries directly. So I asked Ghadirian, whose gentle nature, kindness and generous disposition had attracted many photographers to gather around her,

'Although I create these photographs in my personal studio, I follow social issues very closely. I am surrounded by photojournalists, friends who cover events, some tragic, others less so, just like life'
Shadi Ghadirian

to build a team so they could apply for funding. This was the beginning of the Tehran-based Fanoos project. Fanoos, which means 'lantern' or 'guiding light' in Farsi, is an association of Iranian photographers that aims to promote the work of more than 120 top photographer-members. Its founders, Jalal Sepehr, Dariush Kiani and Shadi Ghadirian, have succeeded in creating an appropriate environment for promoting photographic art and providing resources to potential exhibitors.

While working hard on the Fanoos website, Ghadirian became pregnant. For a professional photographer, digitisation and the Internet are a double-edged sword, and the computer work exhausted her. She assembled her sister and friends, and asked them to perform 'the dance of exhaustion', to perform the fatigue of the computer-bound worker. To Ghadirian, the contained world of the computer is just as inspiring as the world outside, a representation of reality, if not reality itself. It also questions the values of globalisation, of obsessive working and the conflicts brought about by changing lifestyles. By the time she

finished the Fanoos photo project, Western funding bodies had changed their policy, and suddenly grants could be given to foreign bodies to promote artists inside Iran.[5]

CONCLUSION

Despite the many temptations offered by Western residencies, Ghadirian continues to live and work in Iran, and to concentrate on photography. She continuously tests the limits of freedom and expression, mirroring the concerns of her generation, who never knew the more secular, cosmopolitan Iran. Hers is the generation who grew up with the veil, and were the first to experience the Islamification of school and university curricula.

Her work is provocative and enlightening, and explores key autobiographical moments that marked her development as an artist – from her graduation to the birth of her daughter. Ghadirian's body of work reveals her unique perspective and keen aesthetic sense, and her willingness to develop as an artist, from the concentrated stillness of the black and white *Untitled Qajar* series, to the colourful, digitally manipulated *Ctrl+Alt+Del*.

Her dry humour and charmingly staged photographs illustrate the contradictions of a society torn between tradition and modernity – the women in her photographs seem to be simply claiming a right, albeit behind closed doors. In each series, Ghadirian negotiates the tightrope between the personal and the public, confession and art, documentary and fiction. The potency of her images, and the fascination they have generated worldwide, have encouraged many other young photographers to come to the forefront and express themselves.

Ghadirian's work is also closely related to the style that has emerged in contemporary Iranian cinema, which blurs reality and fiction: her photographs, though staged, are based on real social issues. She explores photography's unique relationship with reality, for photographs are true and false – true, because they refer to a lived reality, and false because they are choreographed, planned and driven by the desire to recognise and share common concerns. She captures a moment in time not to reveal fact, but to create a metaphor about life and art.

Rose Issa, London 2008
Rose Issa is a curator and producer specialising in the visual arts and film from the Arab world and Iran.

[1] I remember Ghadirian asking me, about ten years ago, to bring her 'solvent' from London to develop her photos. When I went to an art supply store in London I saw many different solvents, so asked her which one to bring. She was bemused, as "in Iran we only have one type of solvent".

[2] In Iran, exhibitions are open for only a short time, partly due to the economics of art and partly due to censorship – before the authorities or members of the public can object, the exhibition is over.

[3] The Photography Museum has since been renamed Akkaskhaneh Shahr and is now administered by the government.

[4] Similarly, *The Day I Became a Woman* (2000), a film by Marziyeh Meshkini (who is married to the Iranian director Mohsen Makhmalbaf) also refers to such forbidden items and activities.

[5] The Prince Claus Fund contributed financially to the production of *Iranian Photography Now* (Hatje Cantz, 2008).

'I tried to reconstruct the atmosphere of that
were chosen from my family and friends, wear
carrying objects that don't belong to my era
made by these women; an act of rebellion, of

era by using familiar backdrops. My models
ing clothes from the turn of the 20th century,
The photographs depict conscious choices
subtlety, of changes foreseen' Shadi Ghadirian

UNTITLED QAJAR SERIES
1998-99

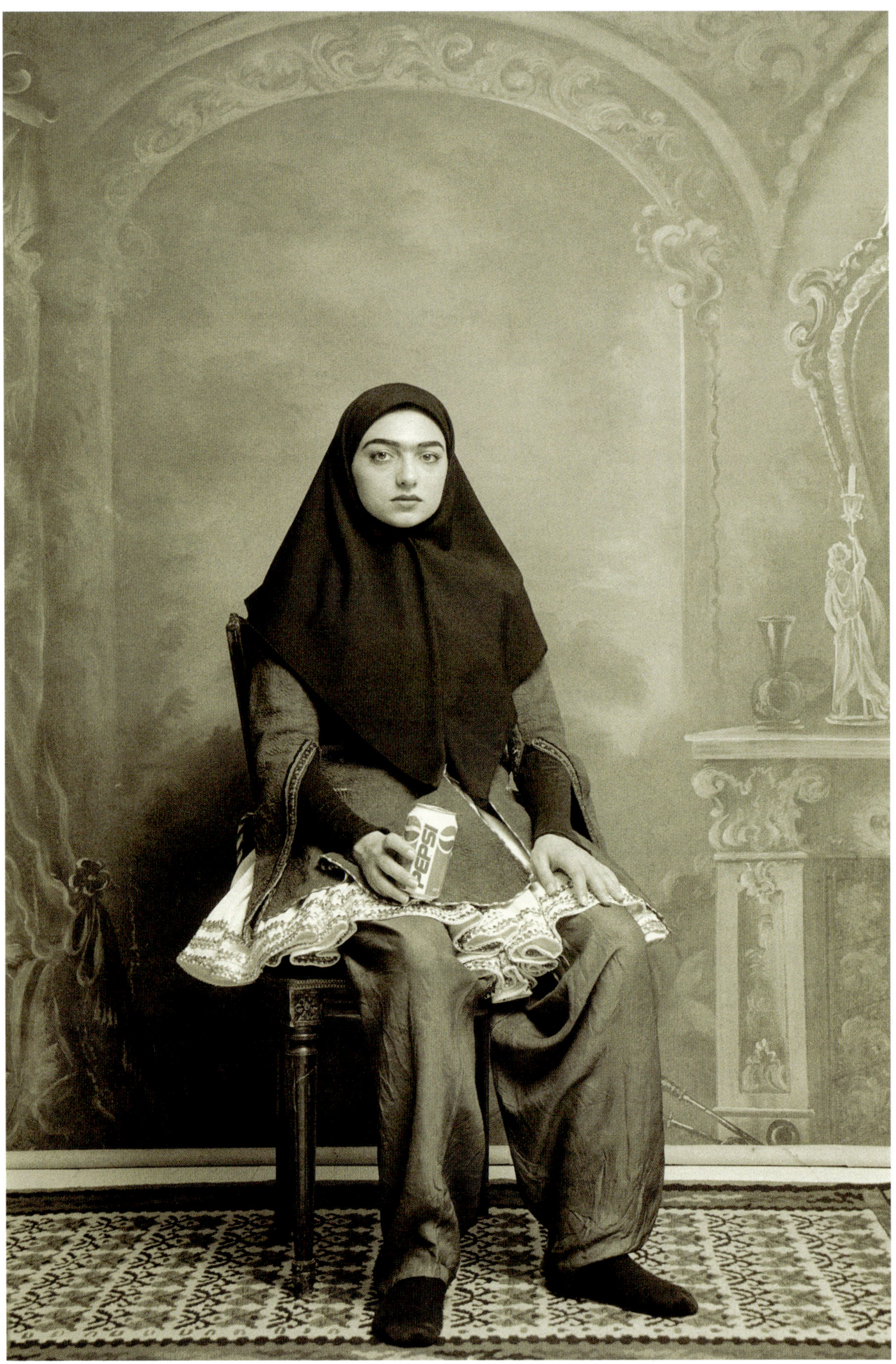

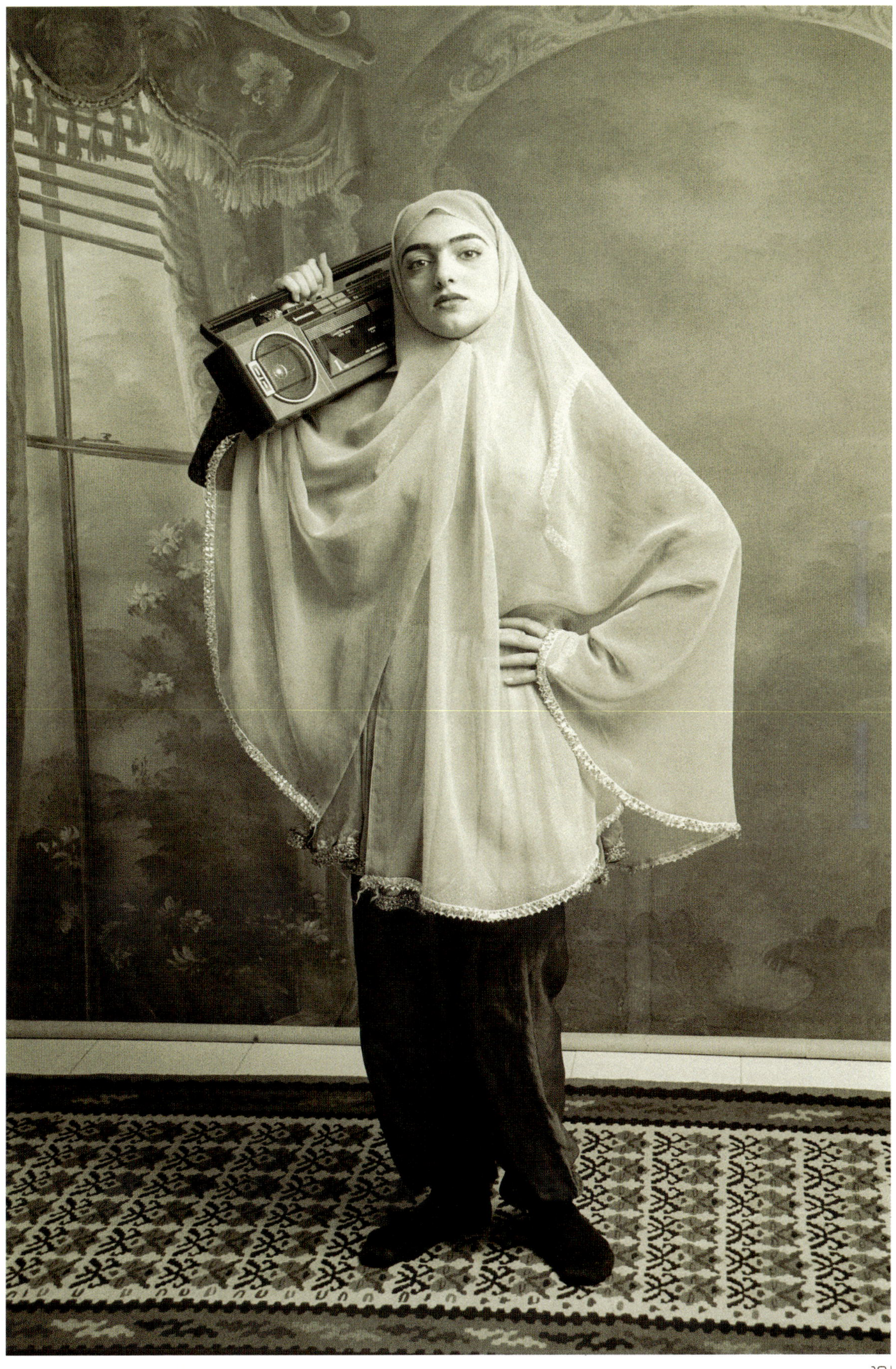

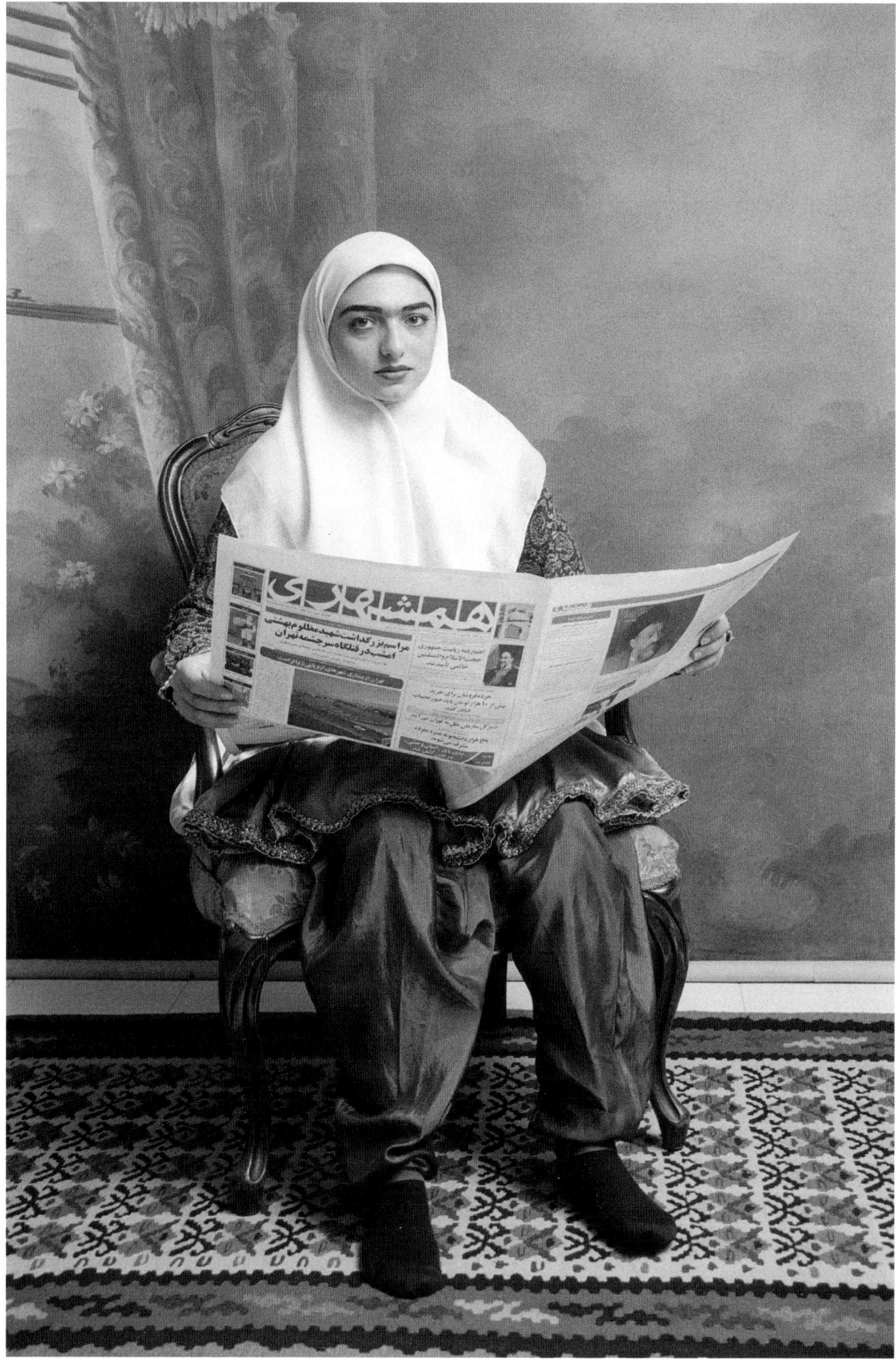

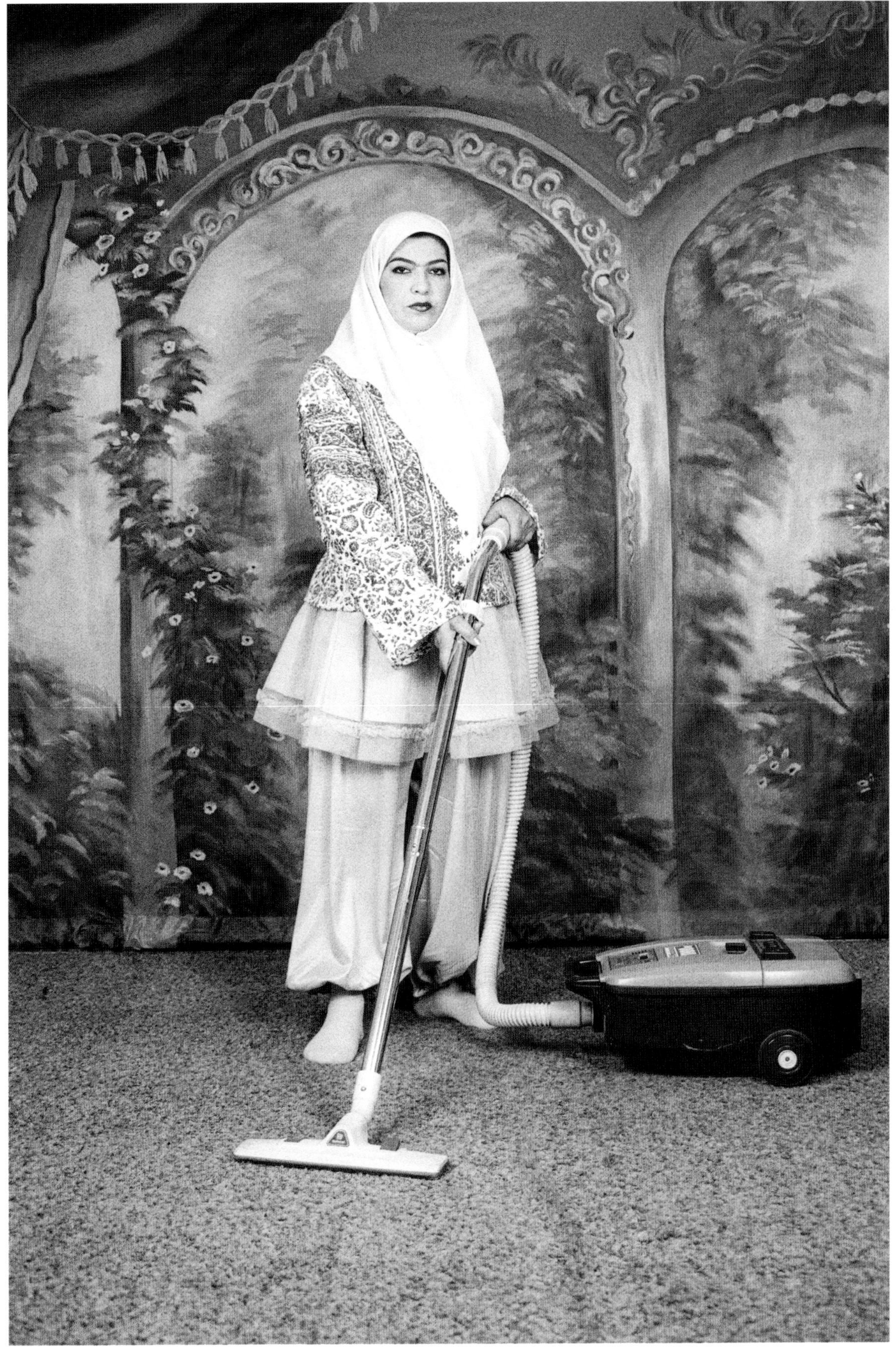

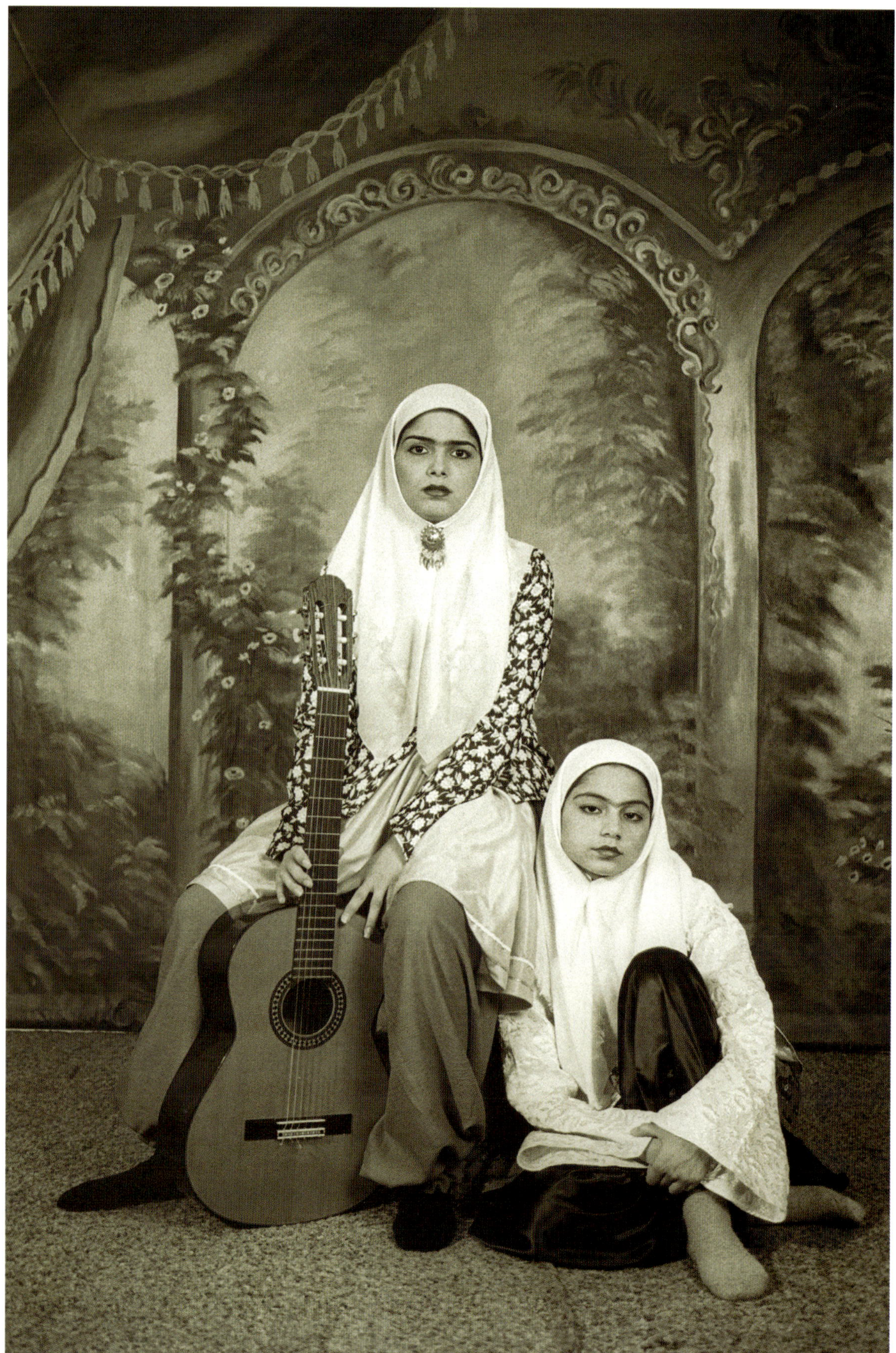

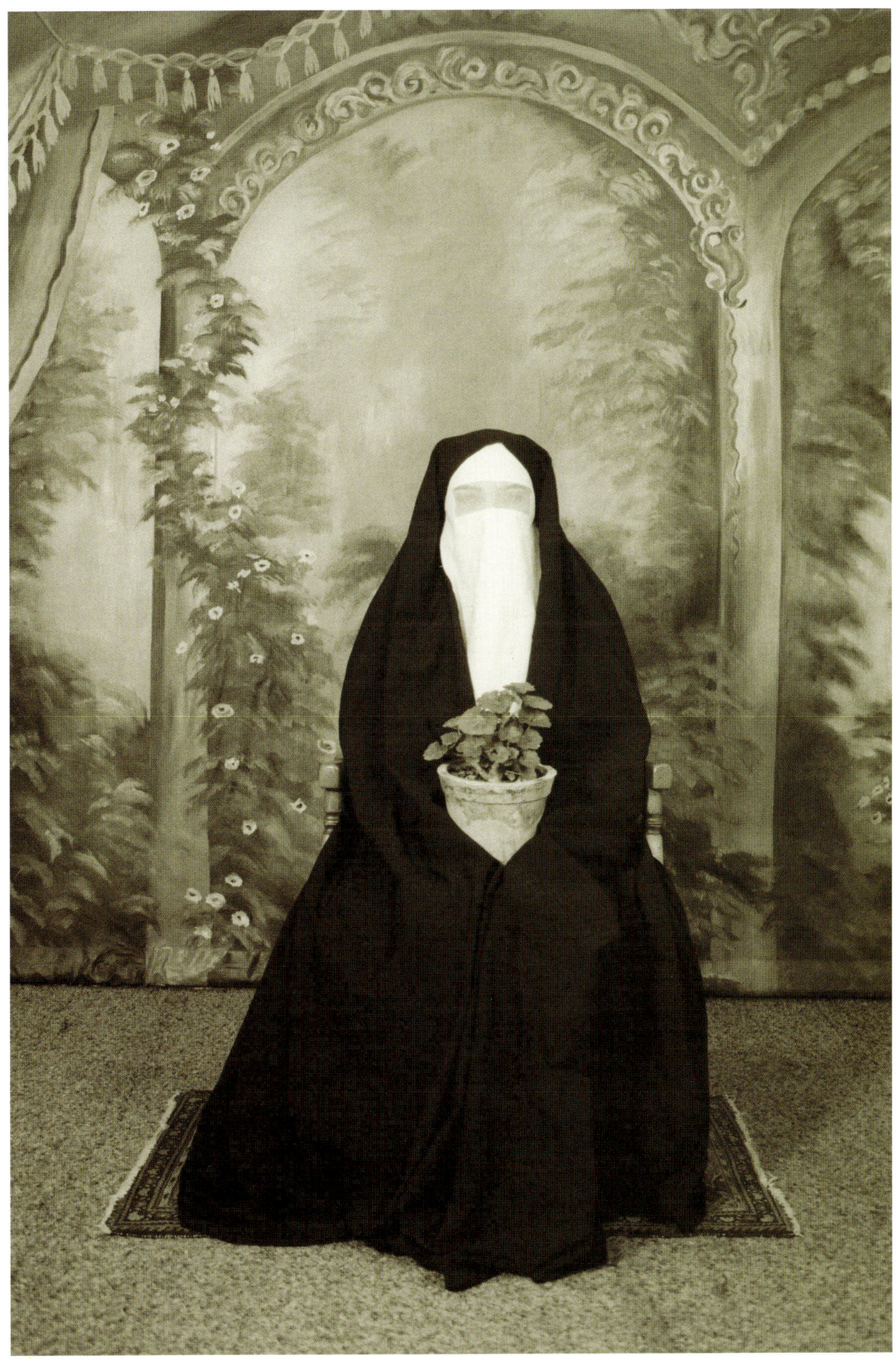

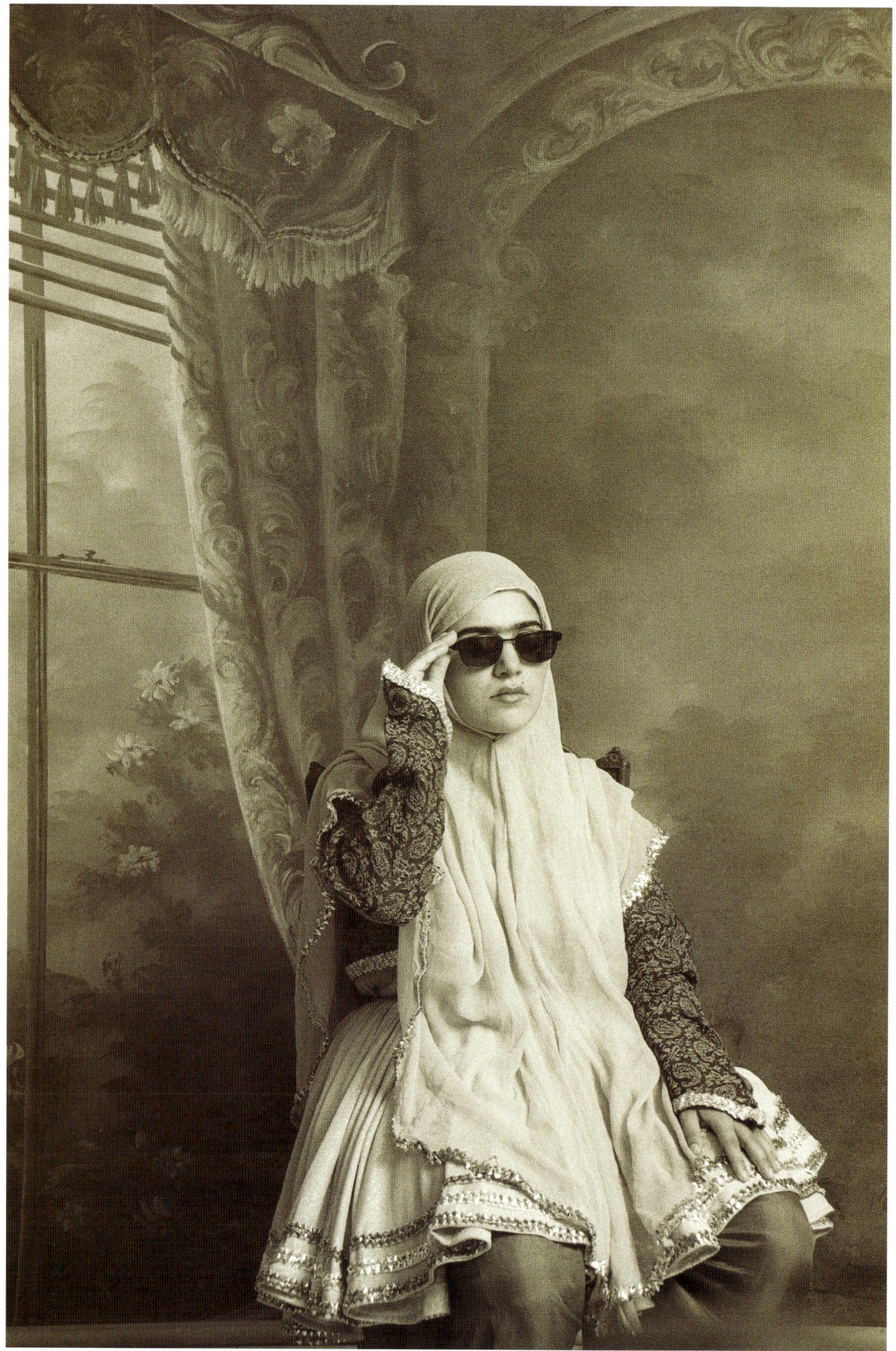

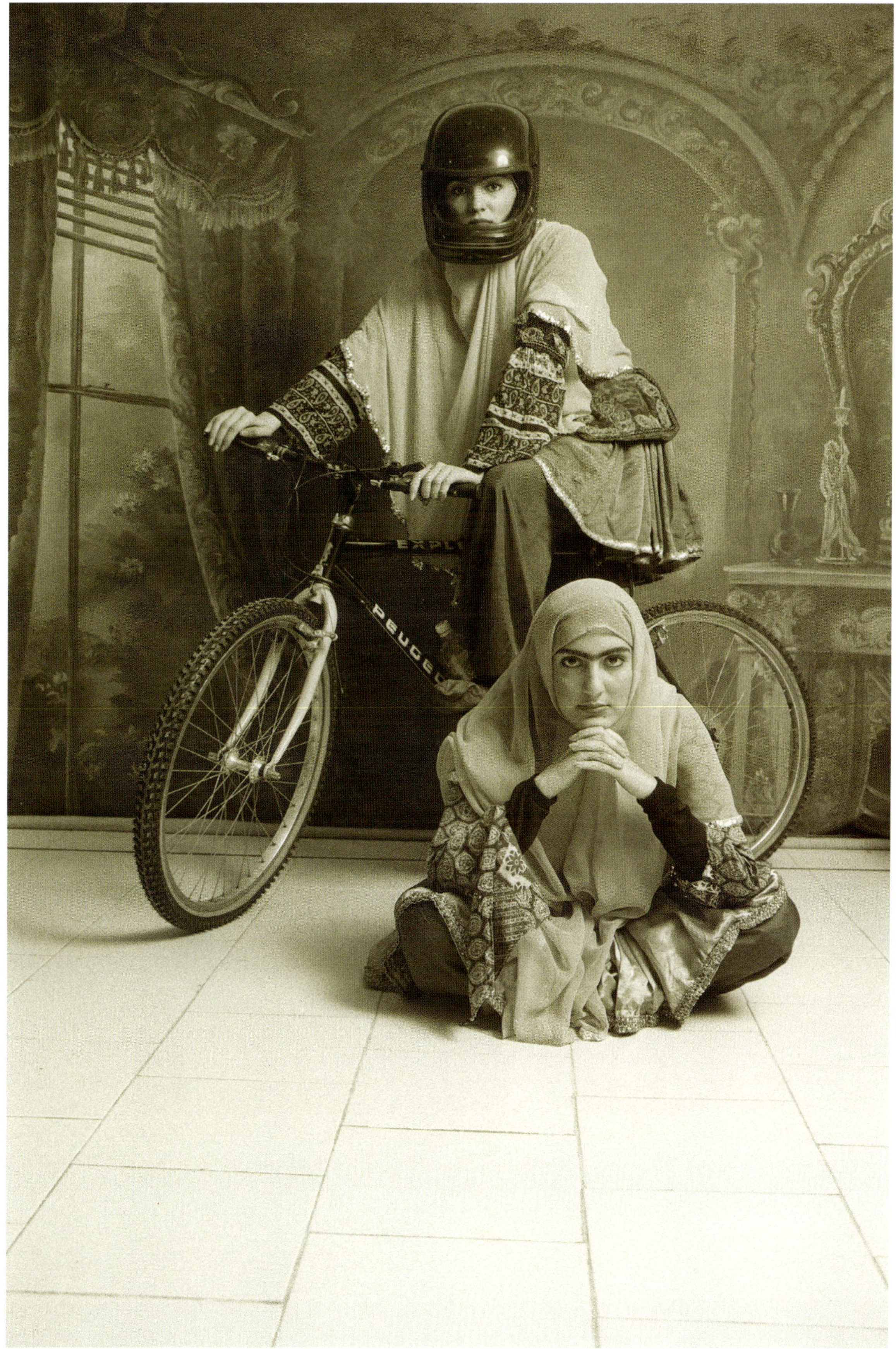

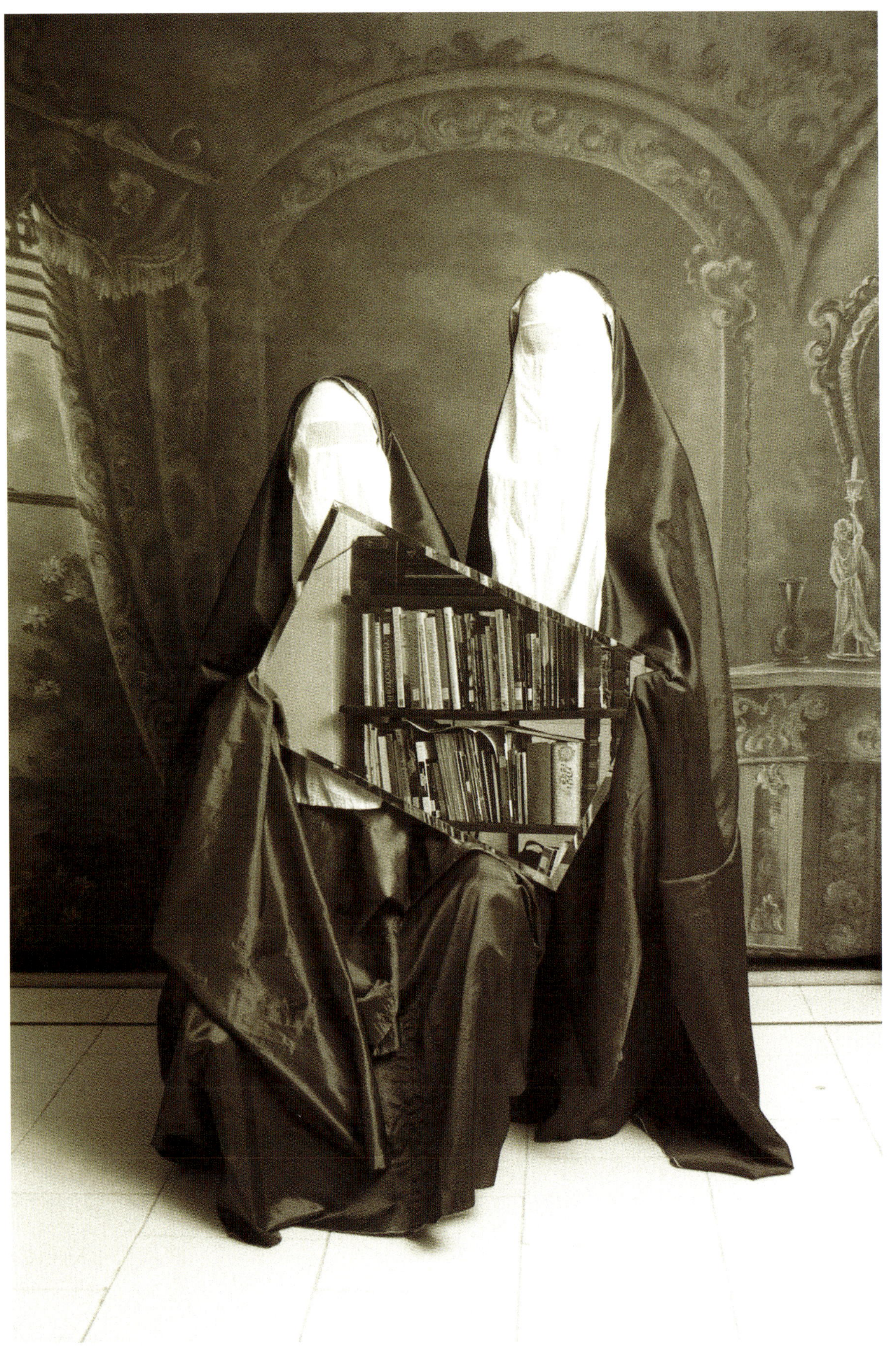

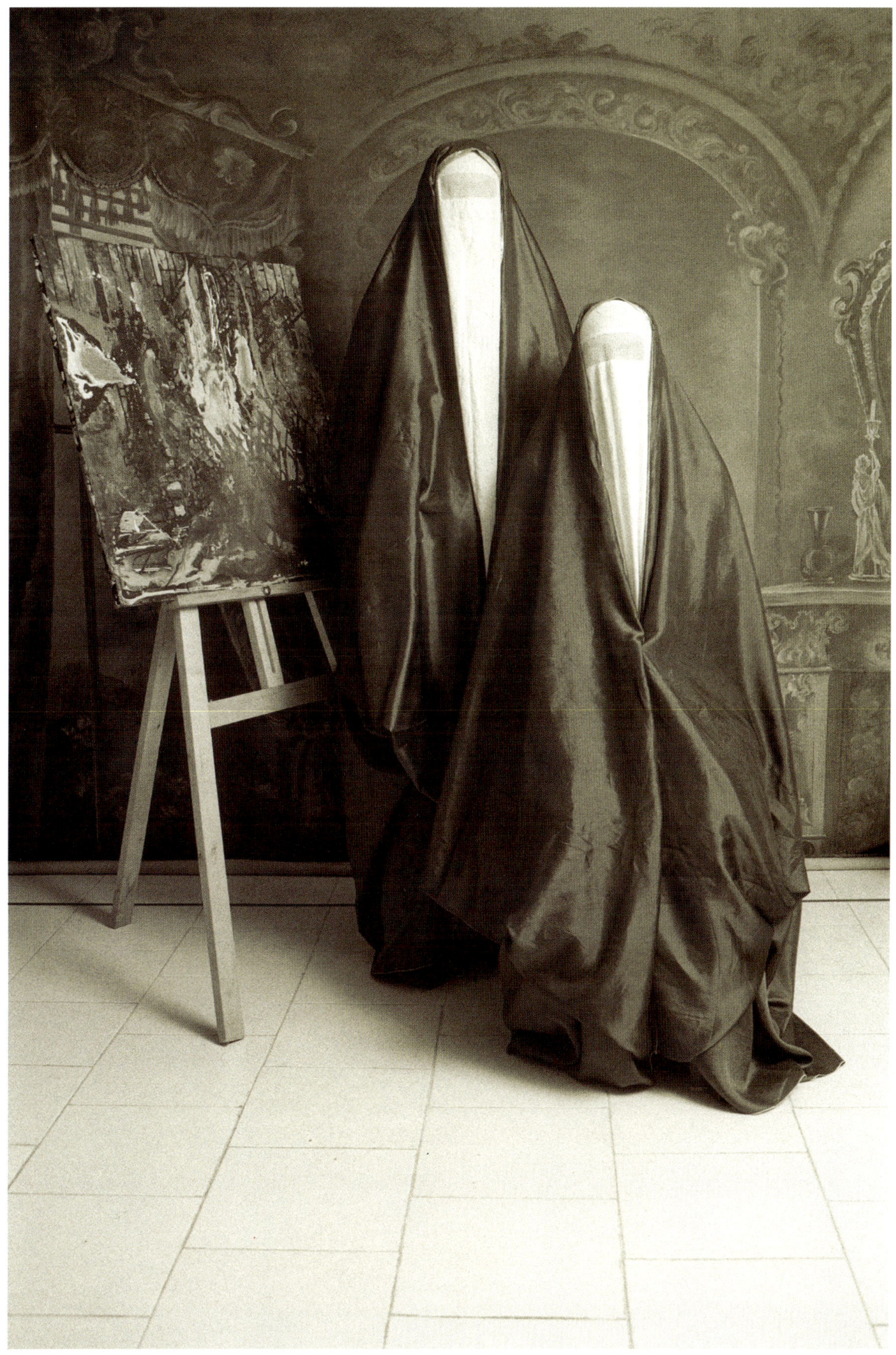

LIKE EVERY DAY SERIES
2001-02

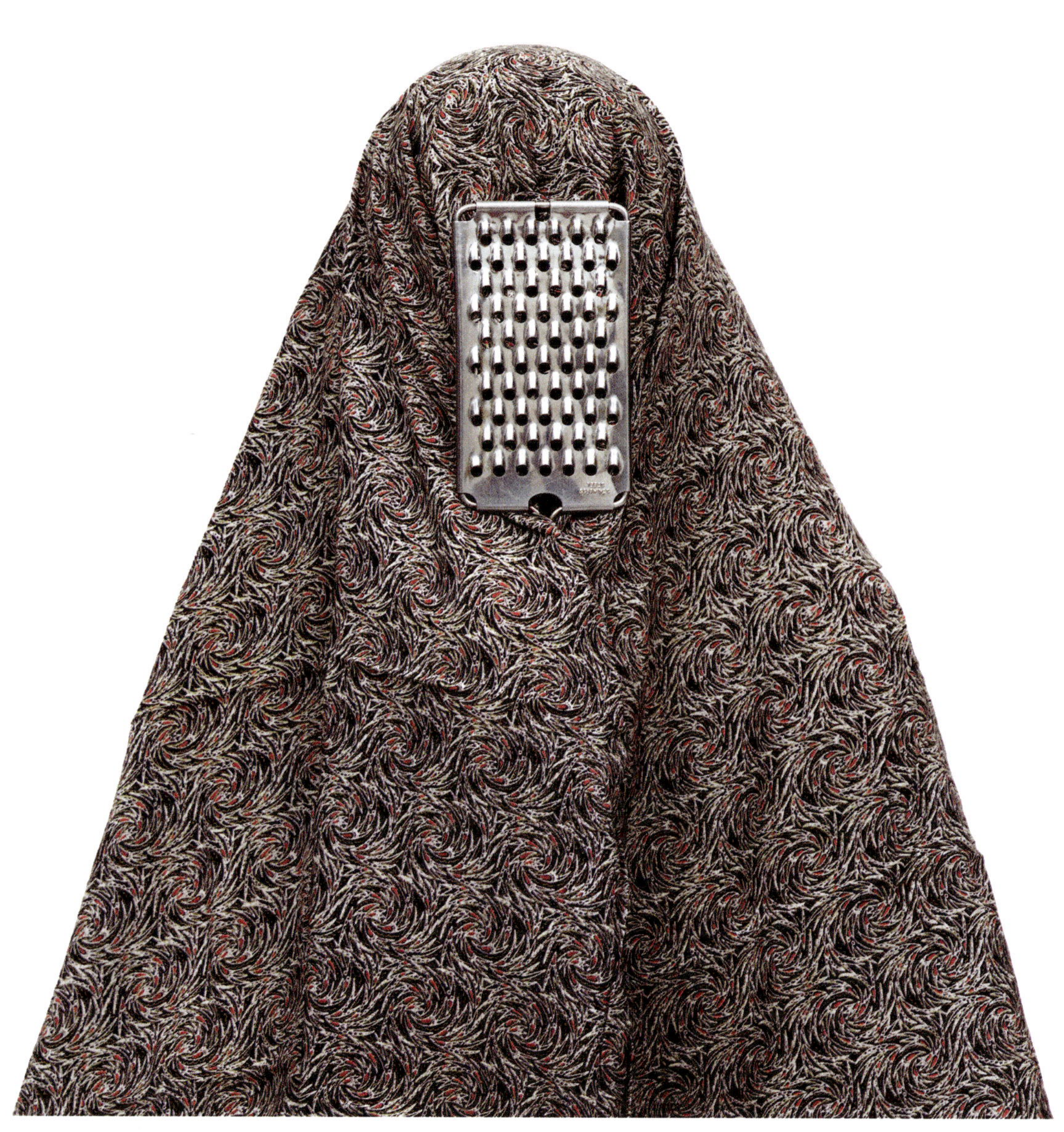

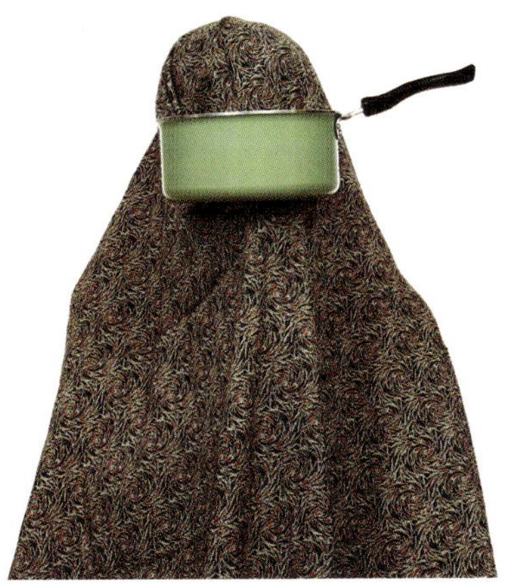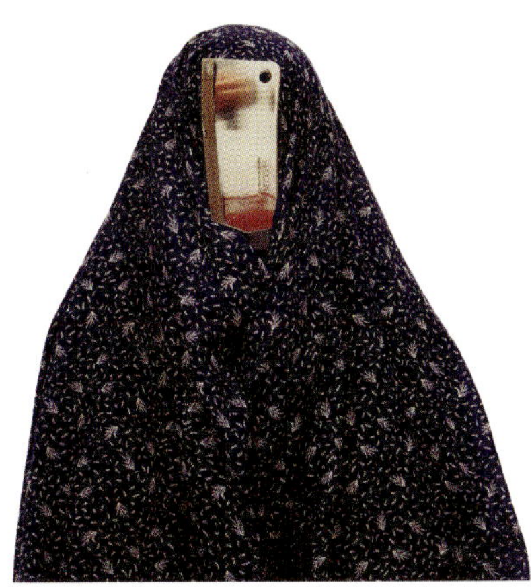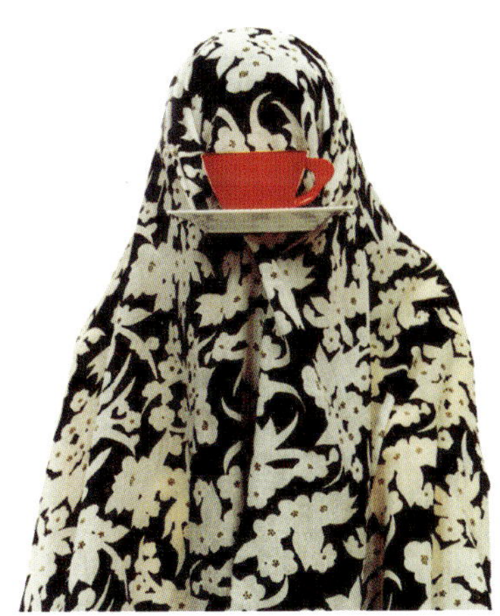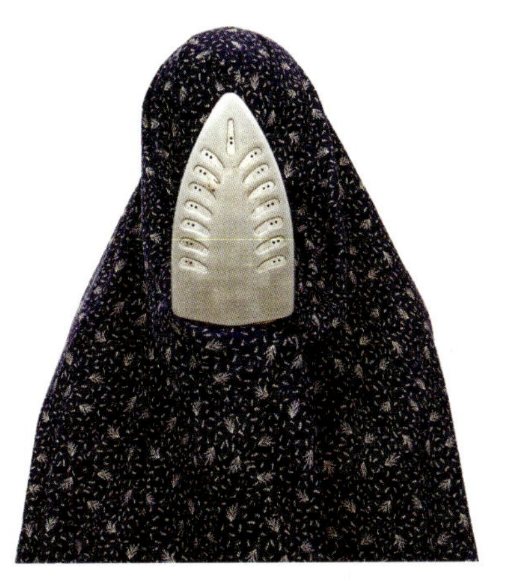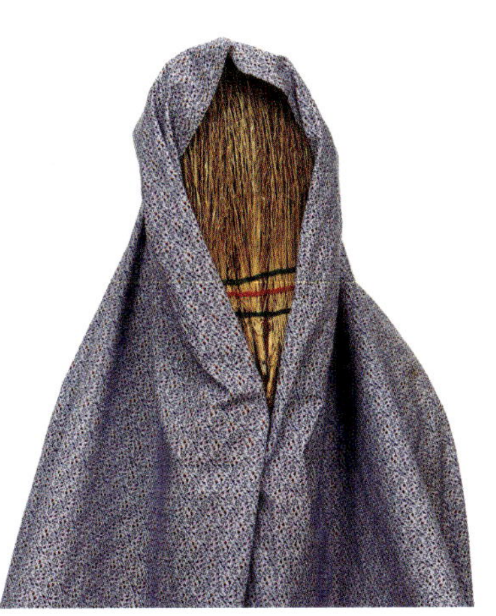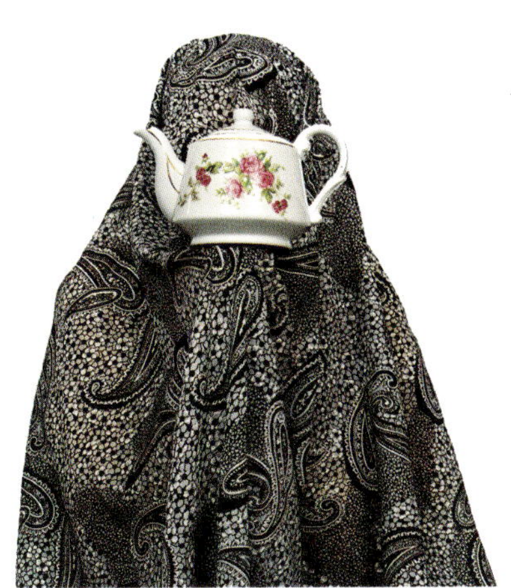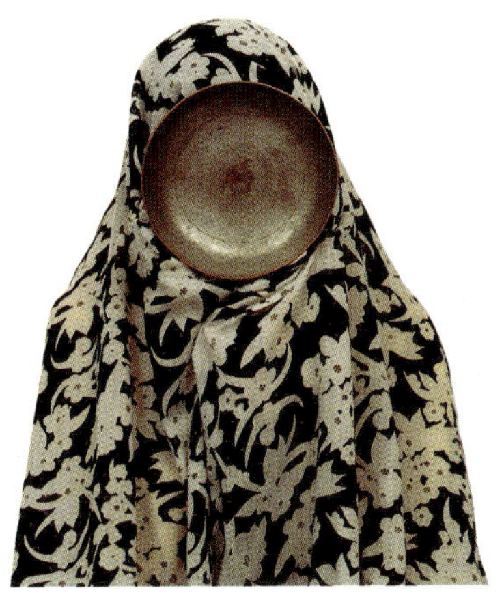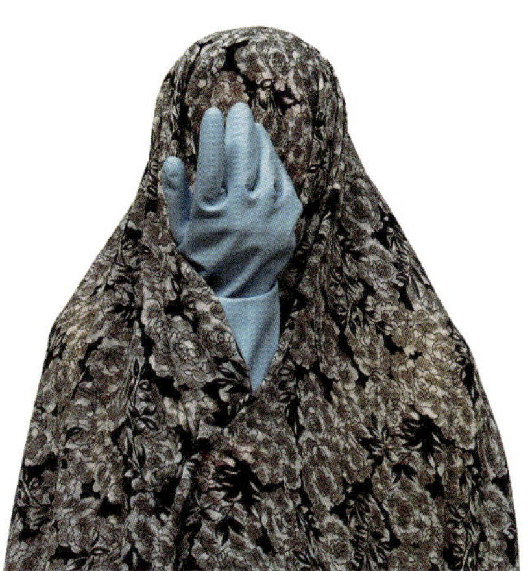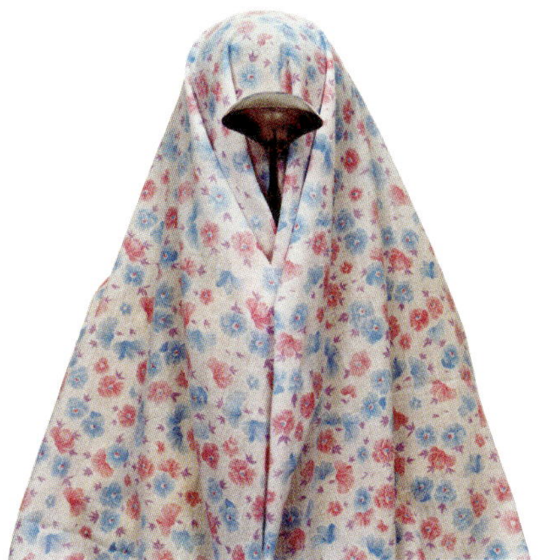

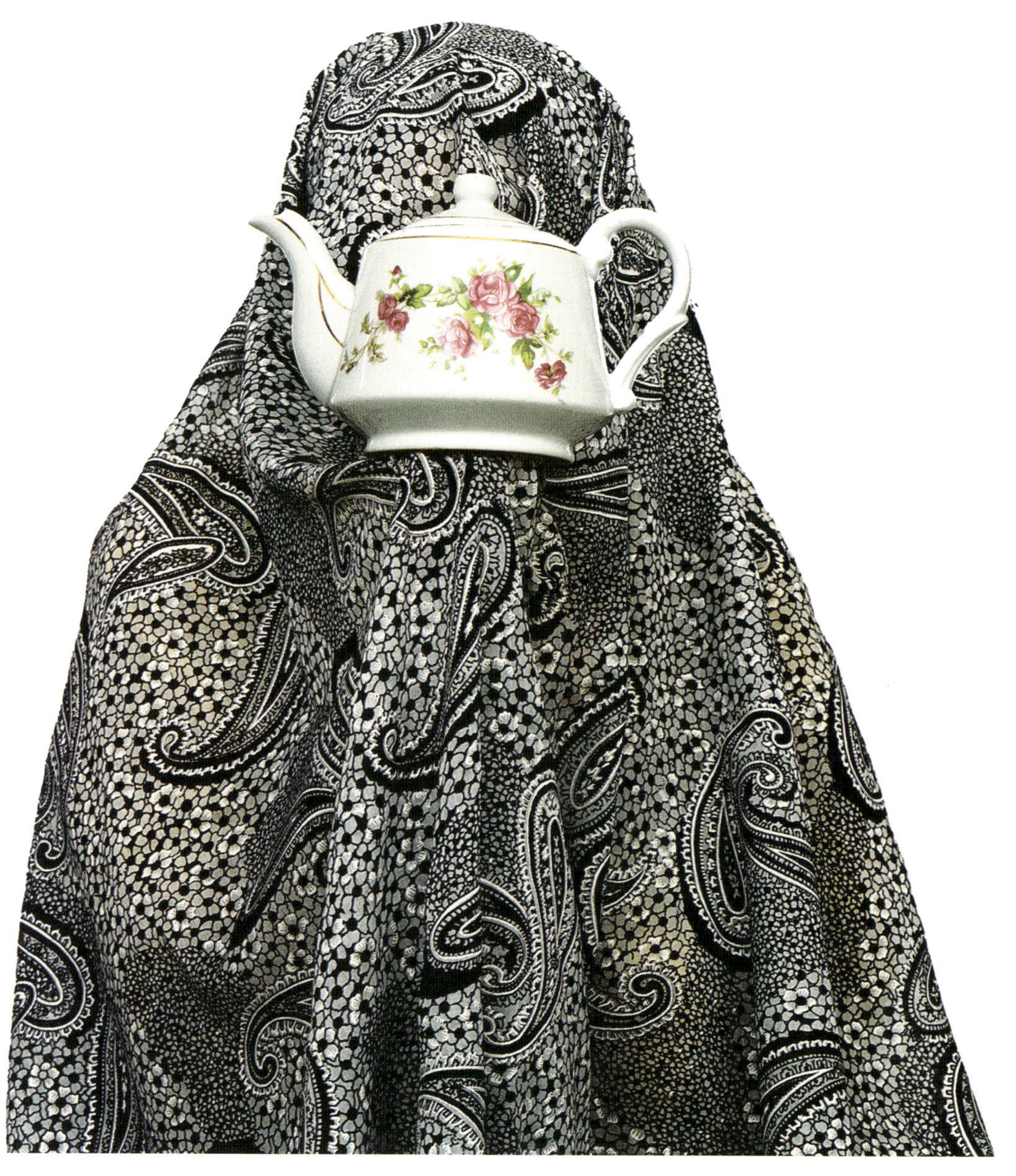

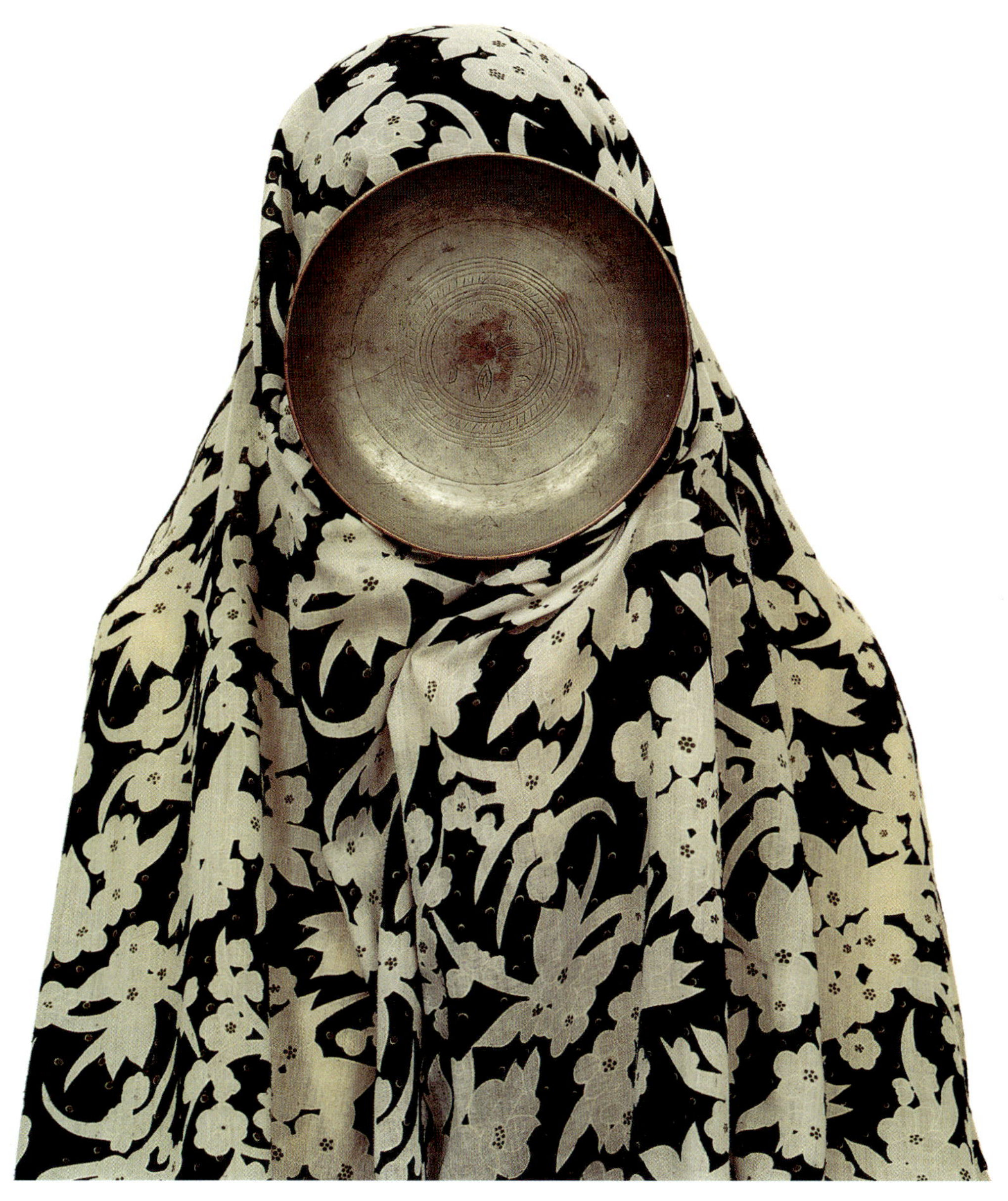

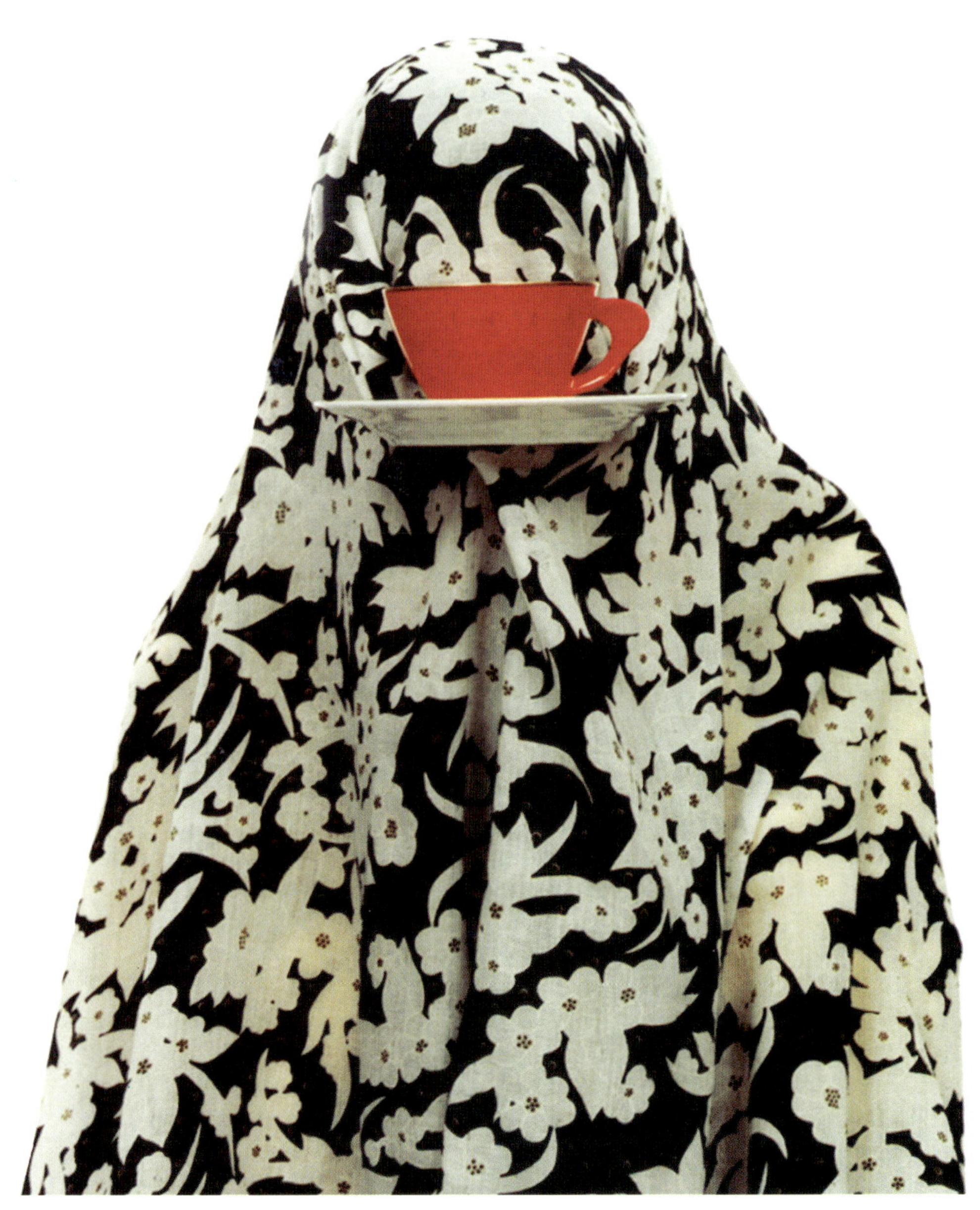

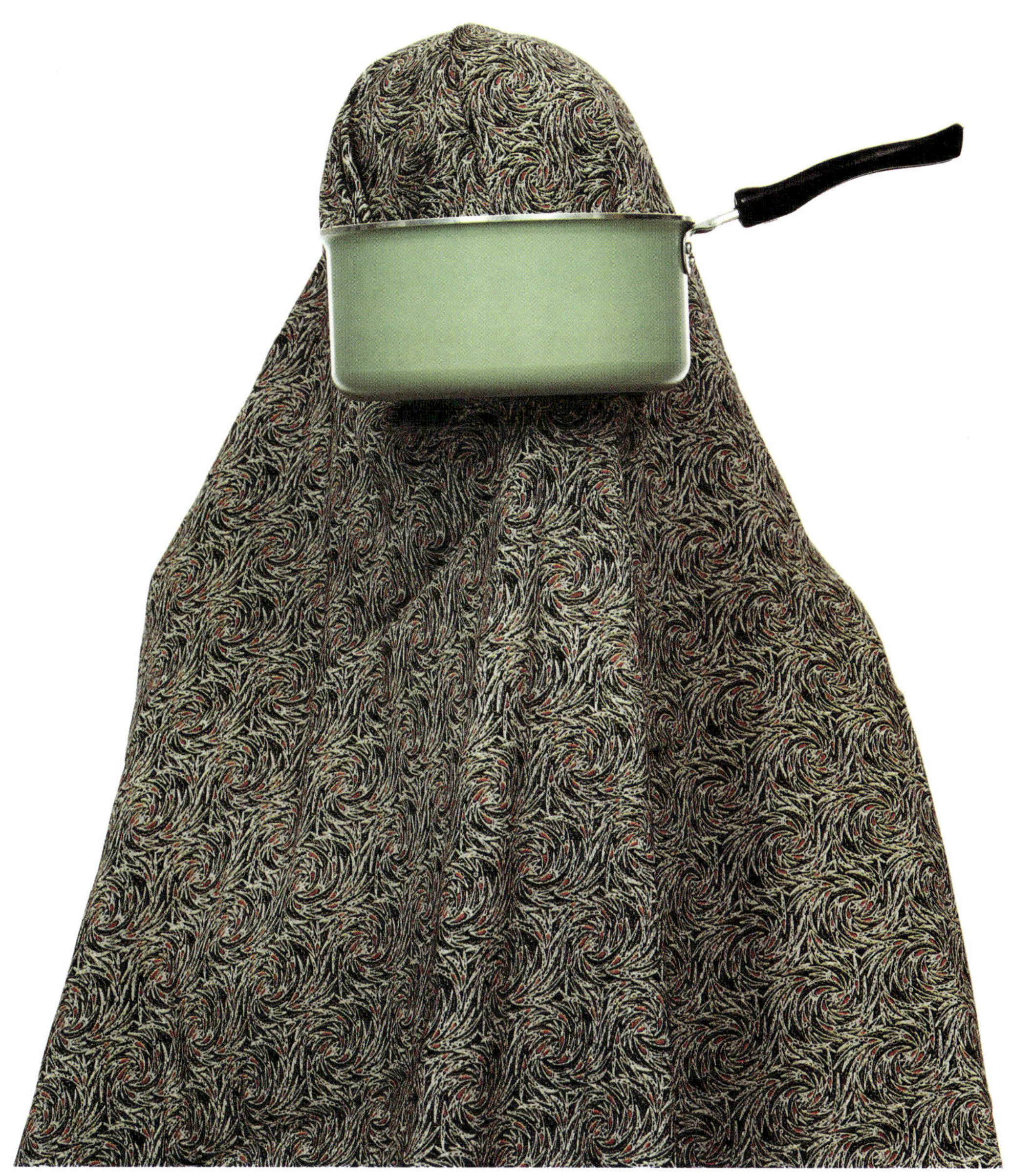

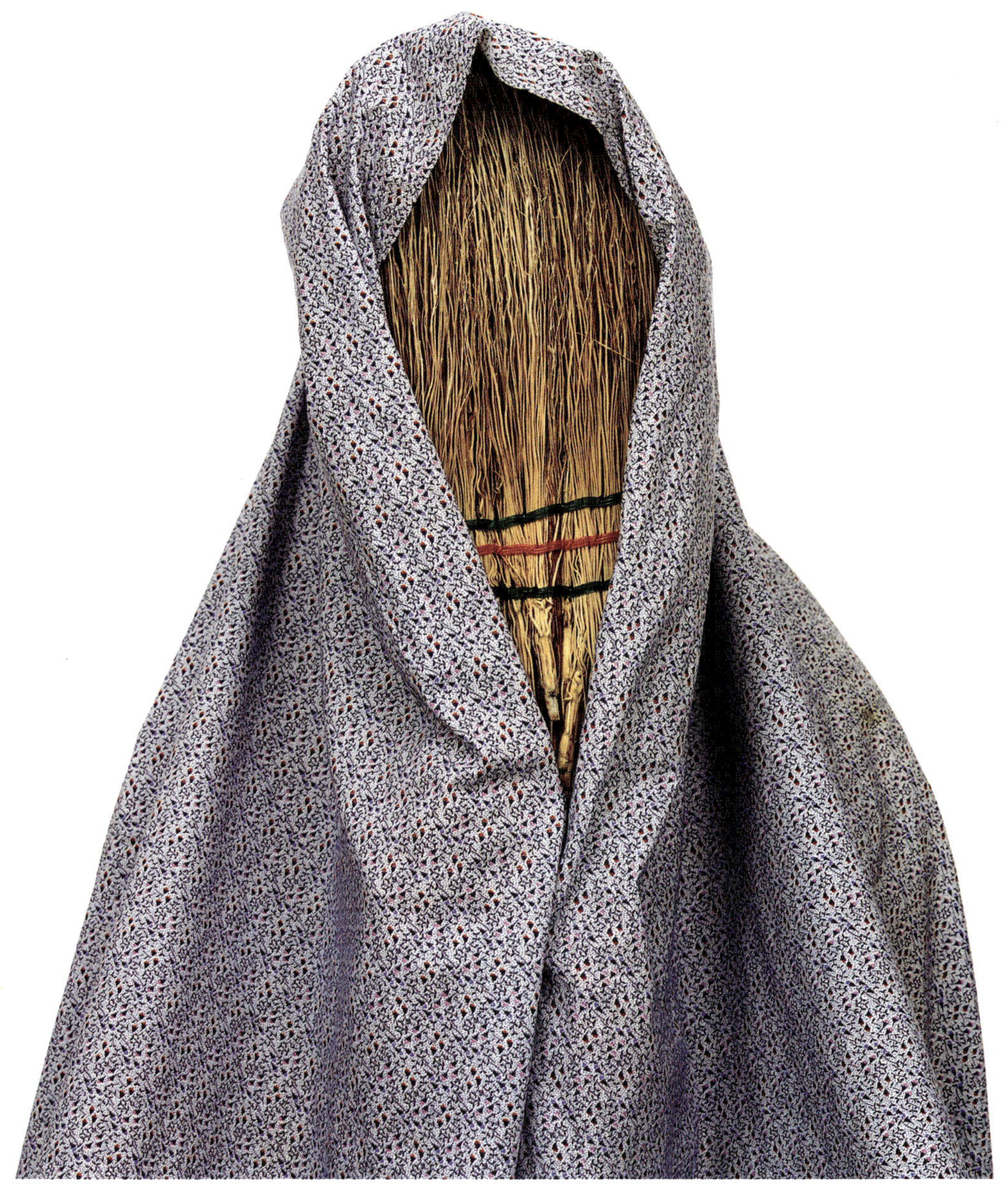

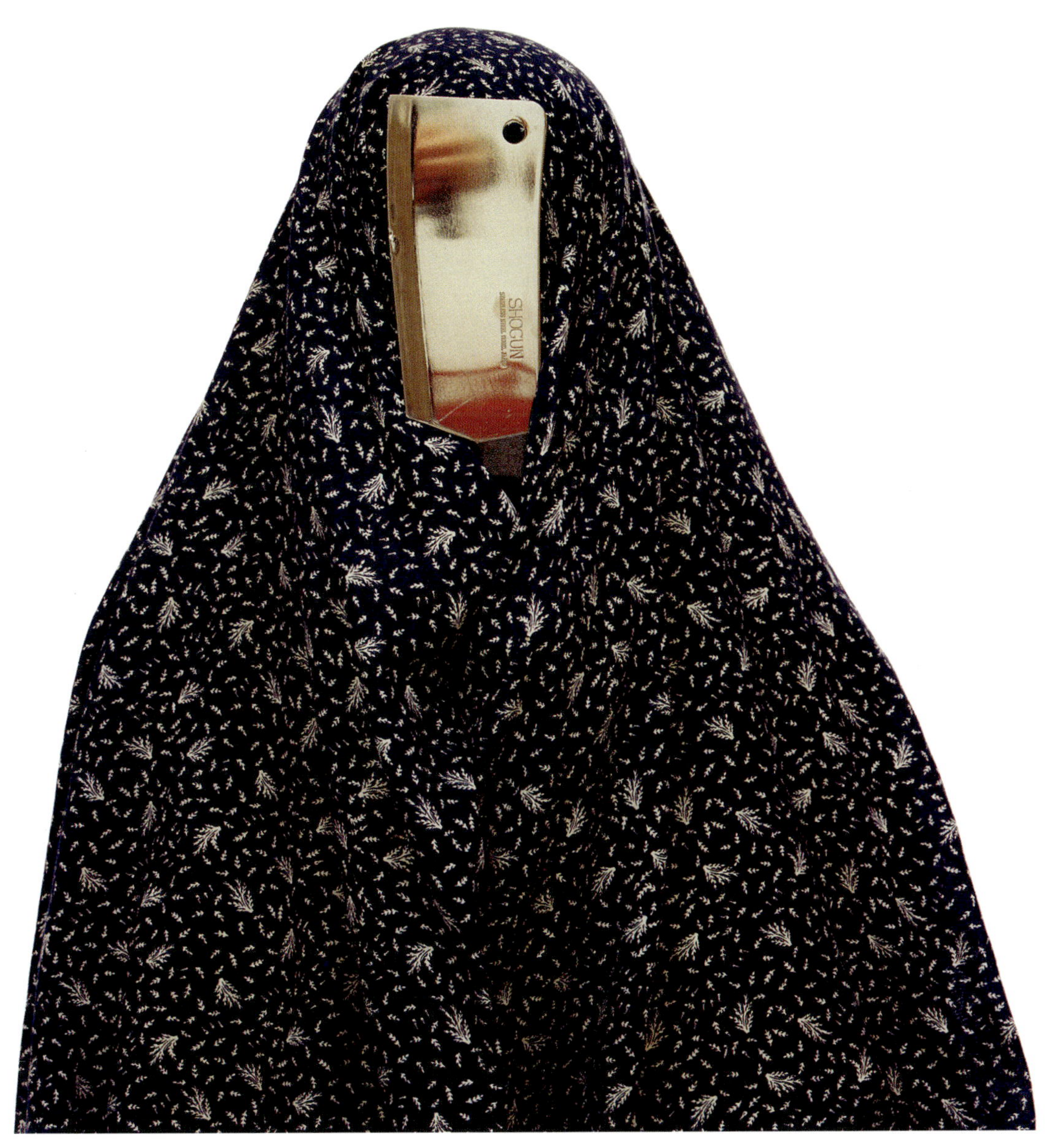

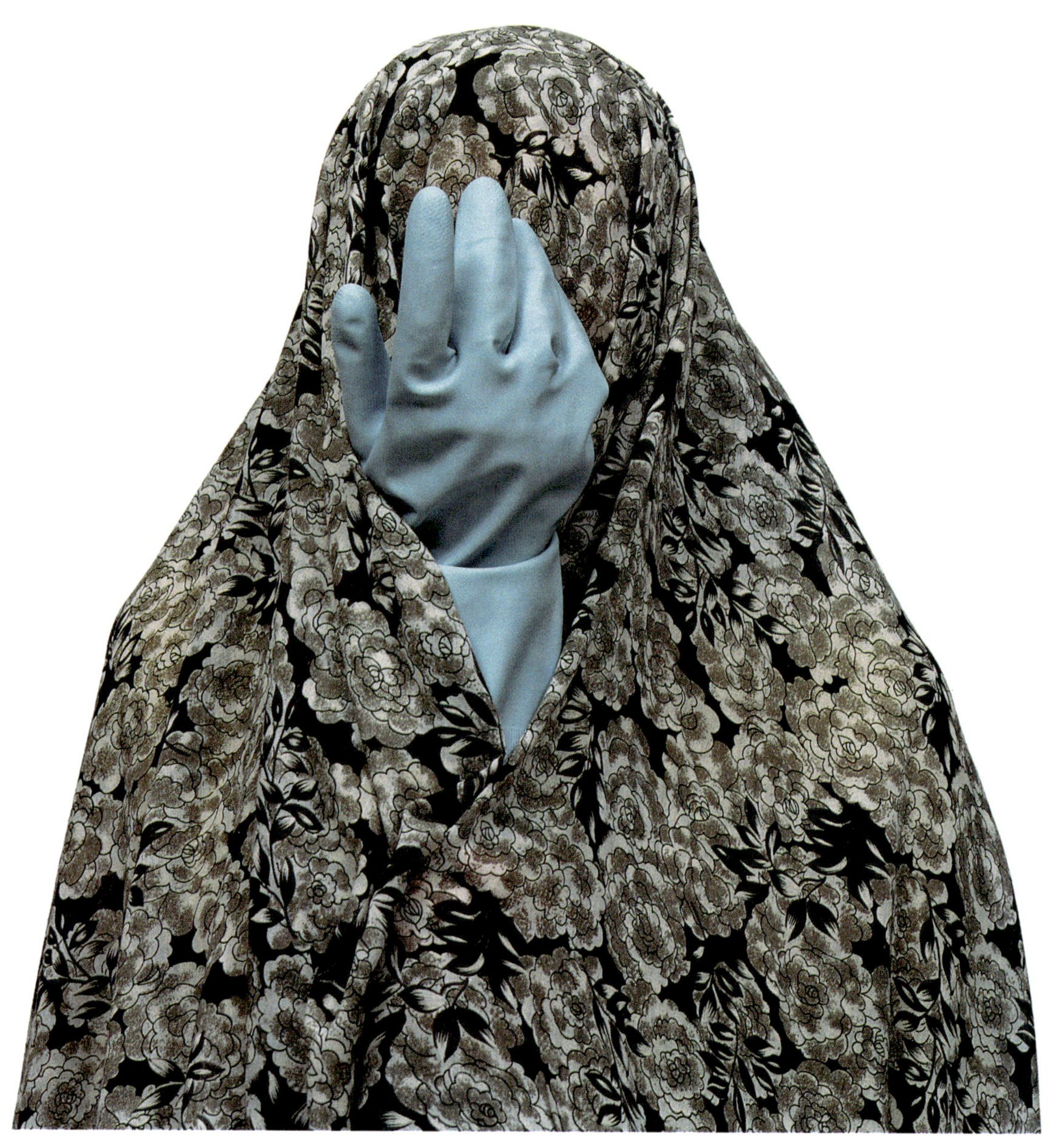

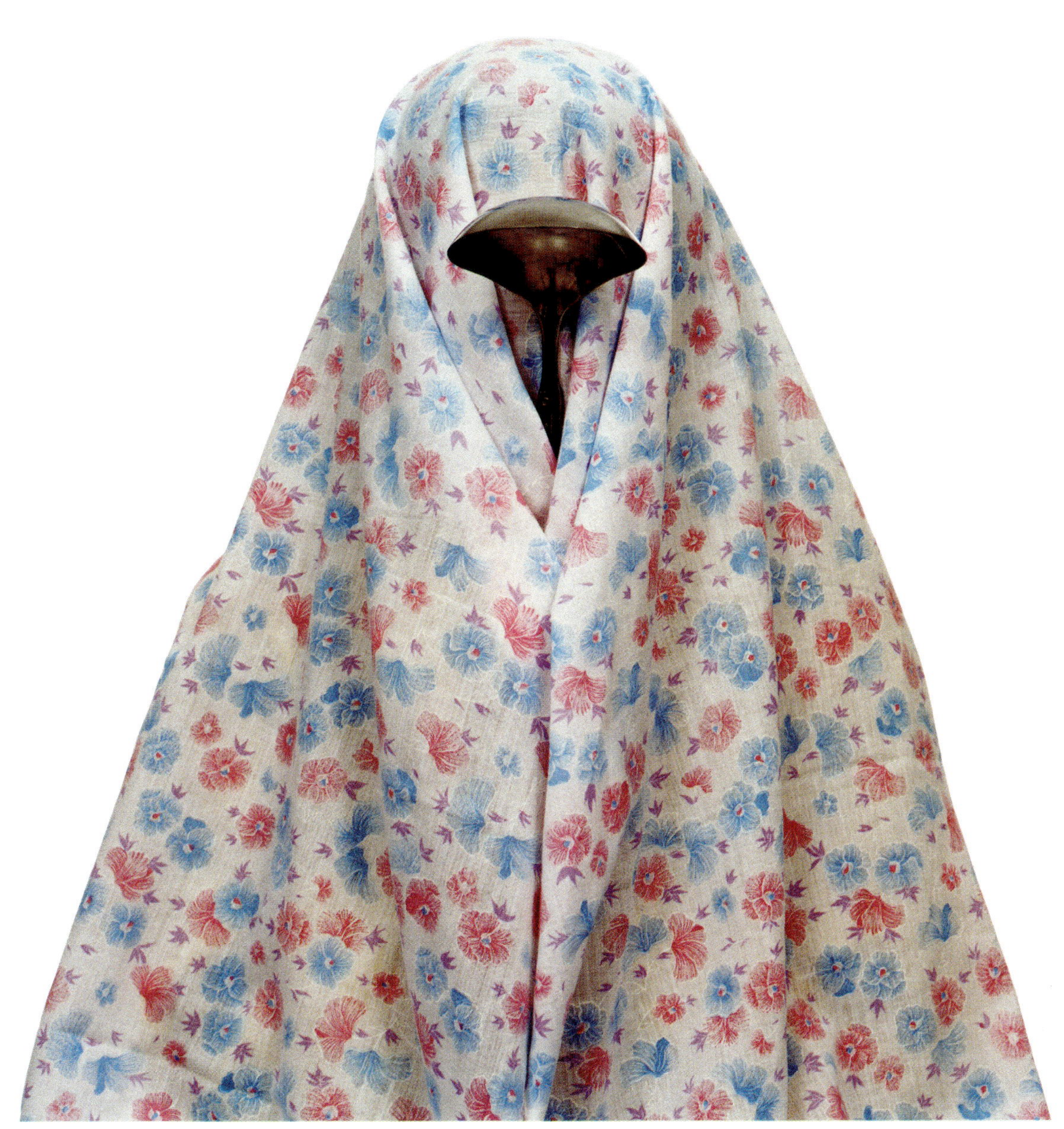

CENSORS' SERIES
2003-04

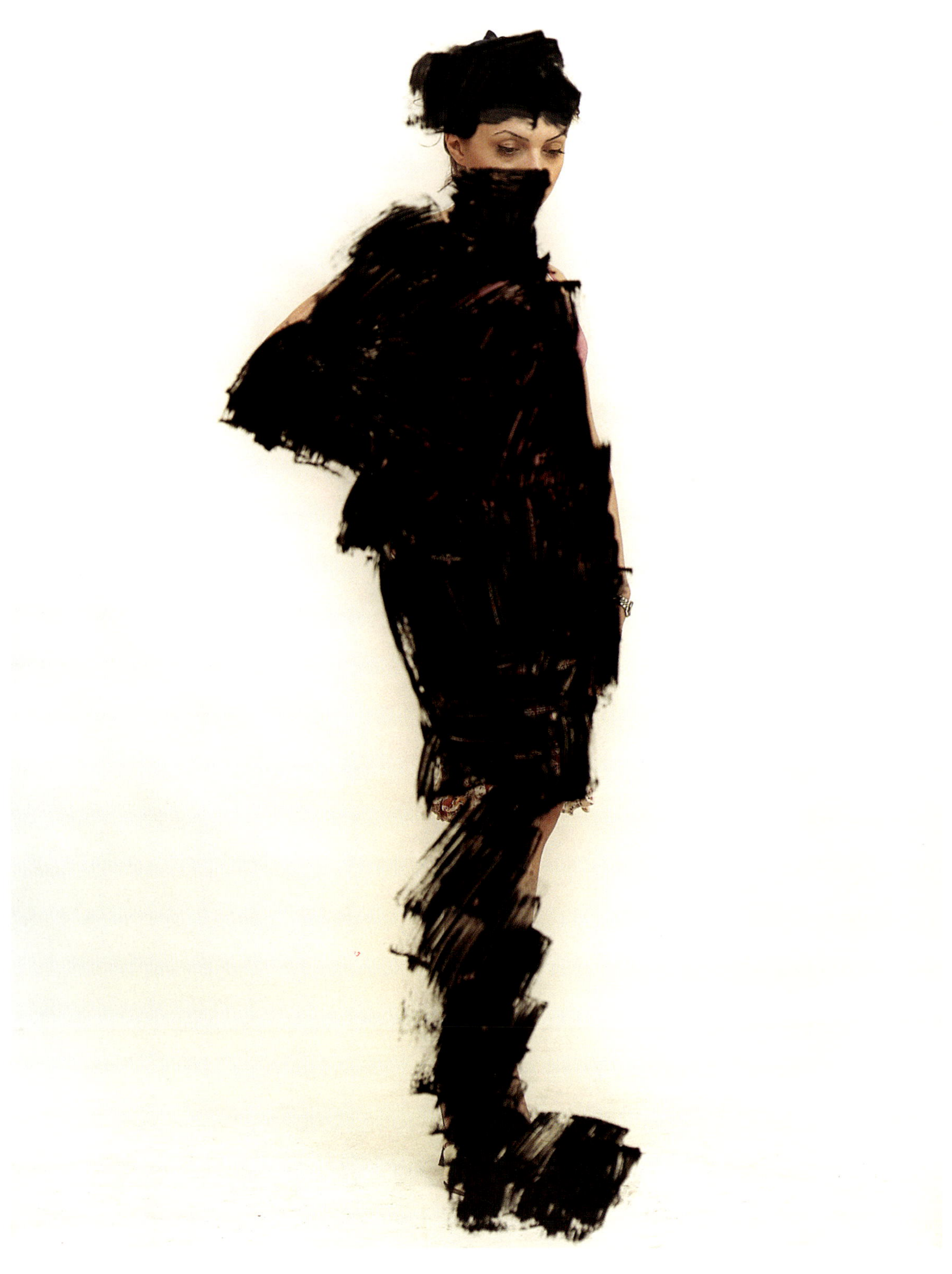

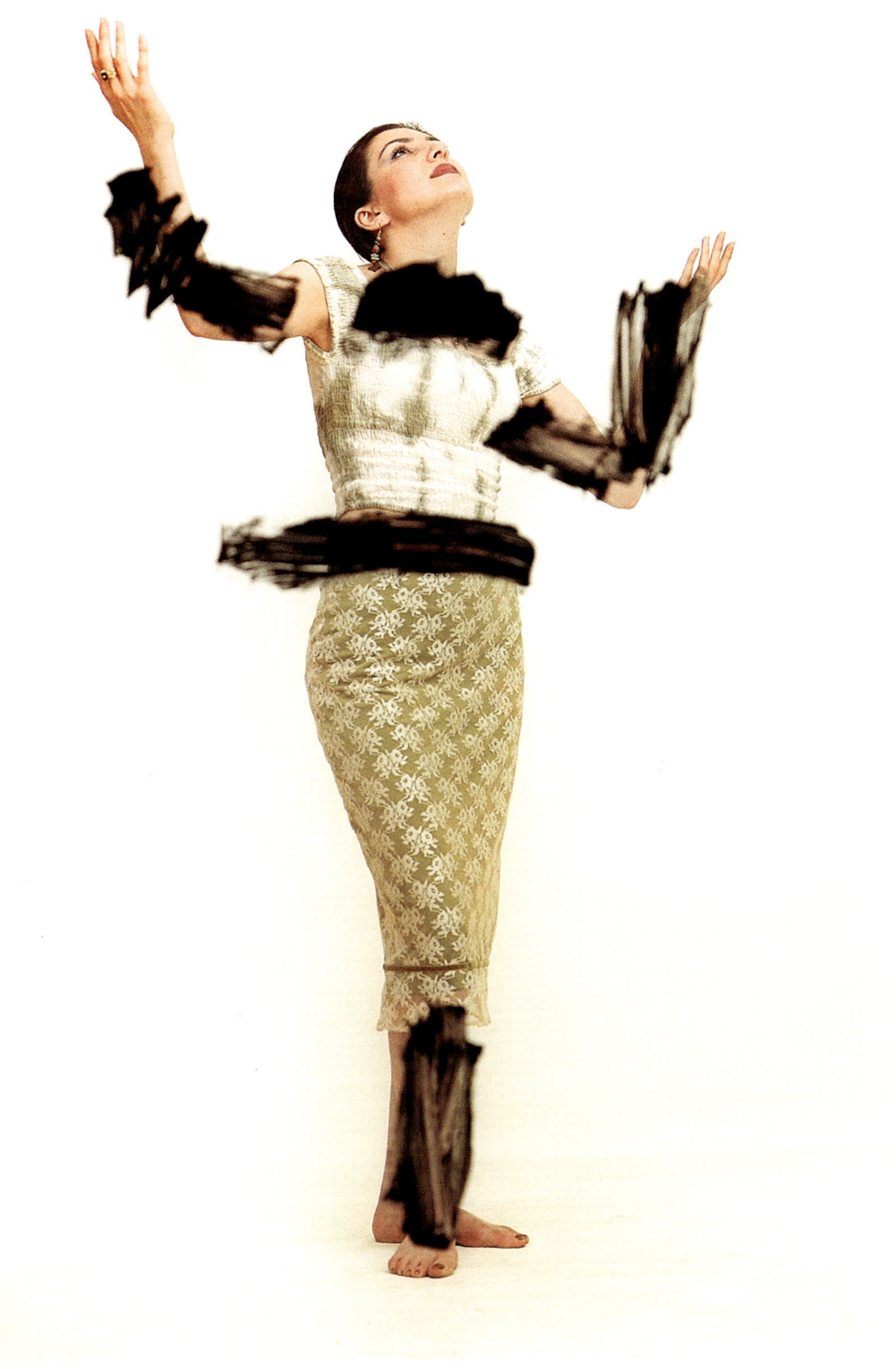

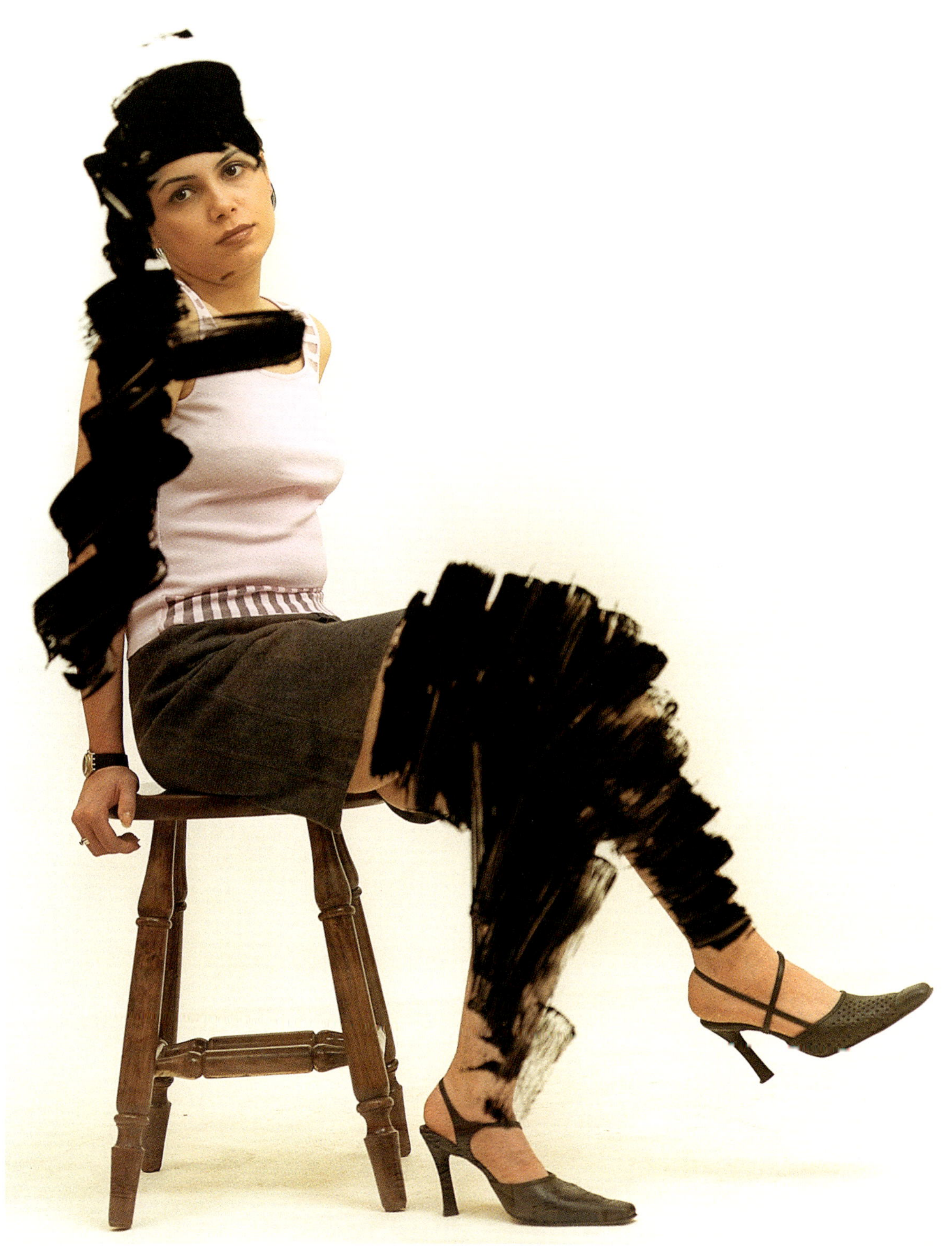

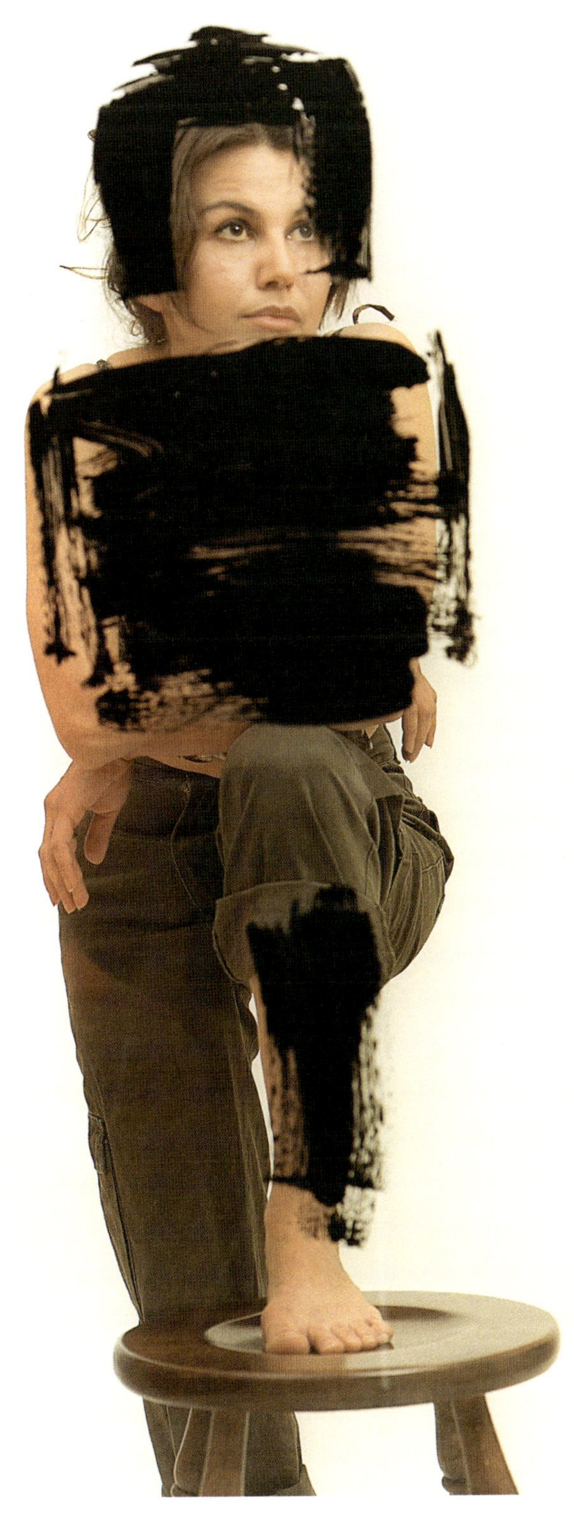

BE COLOURFUL SERIES
2004-05

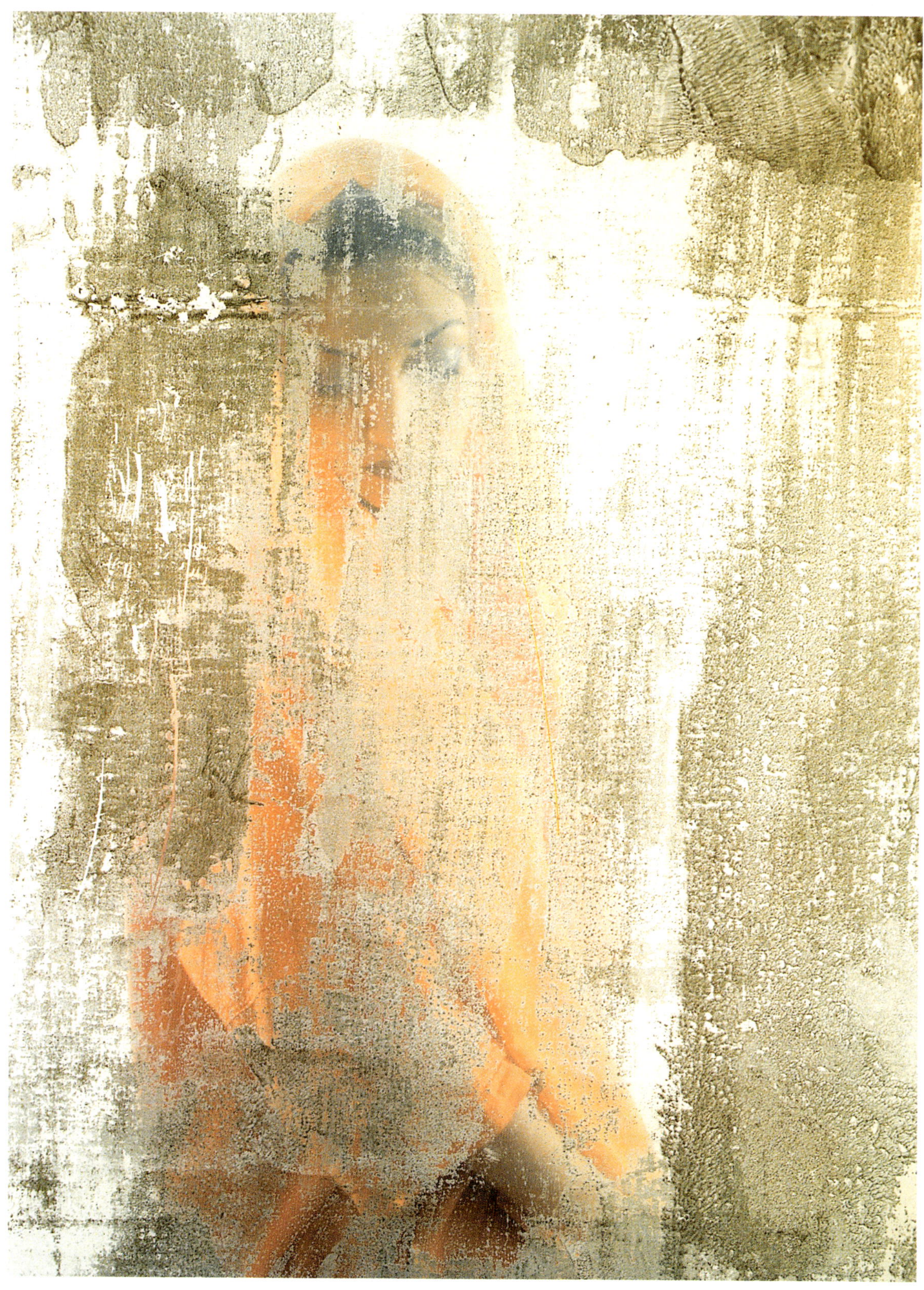

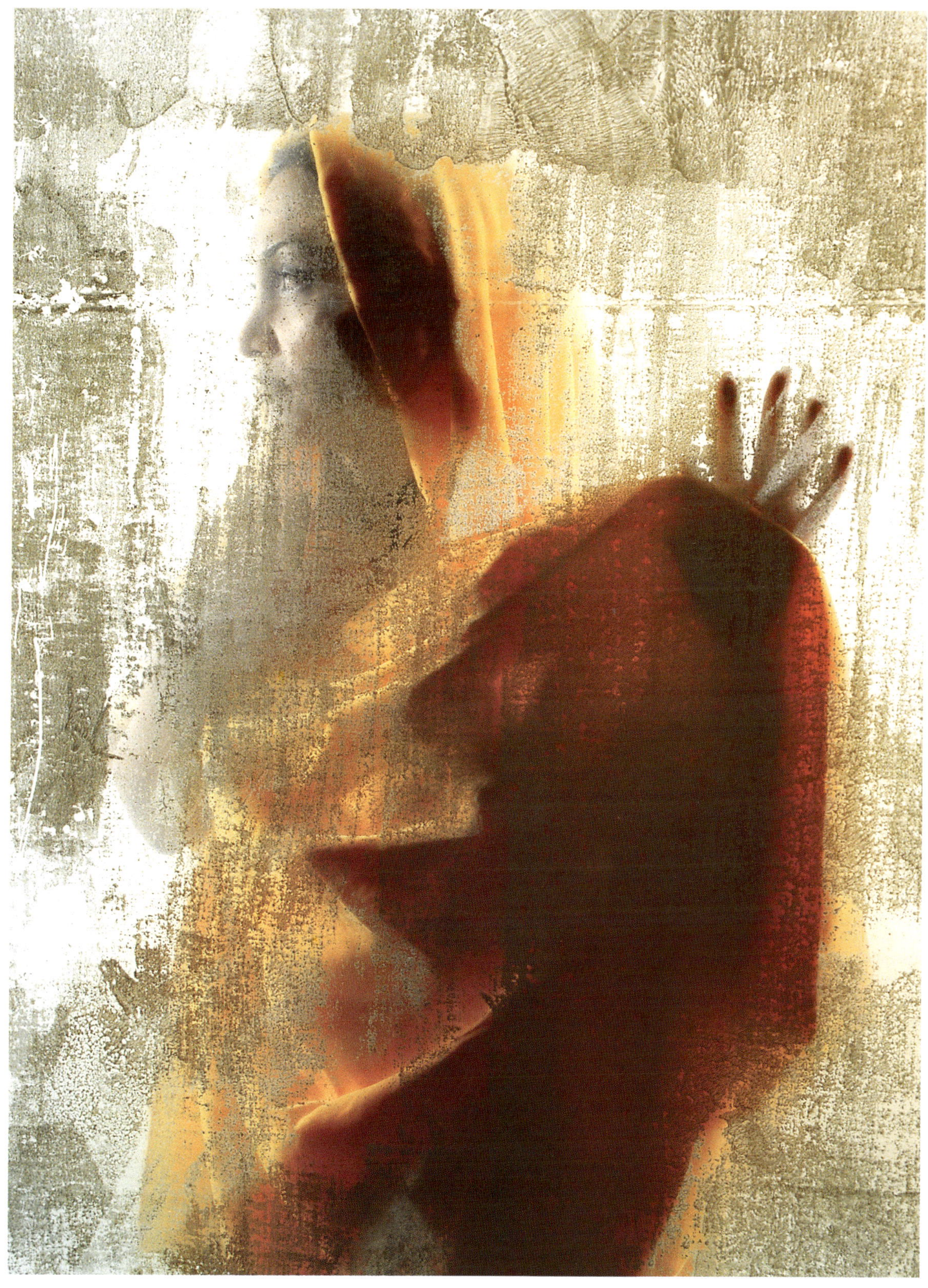

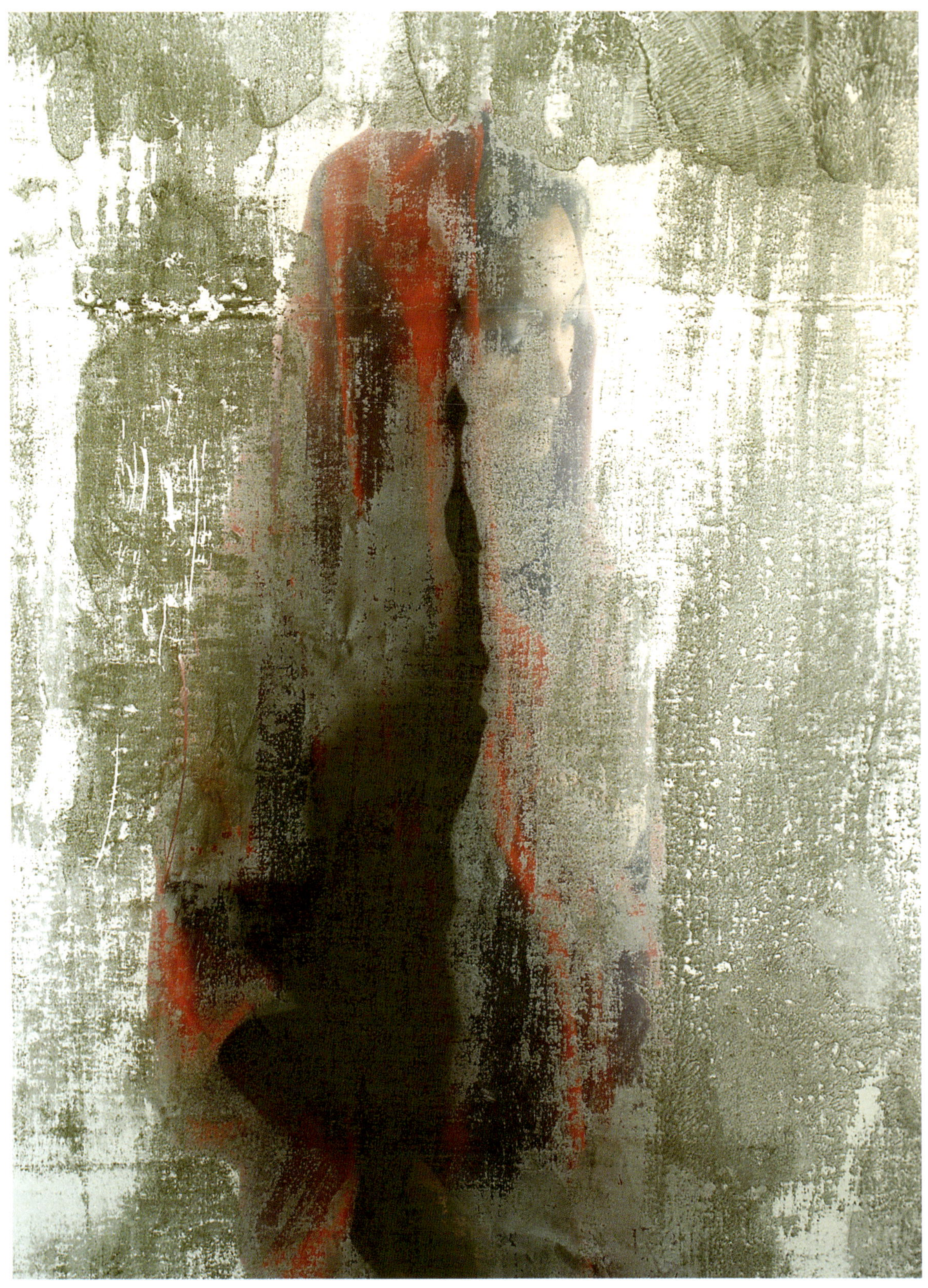

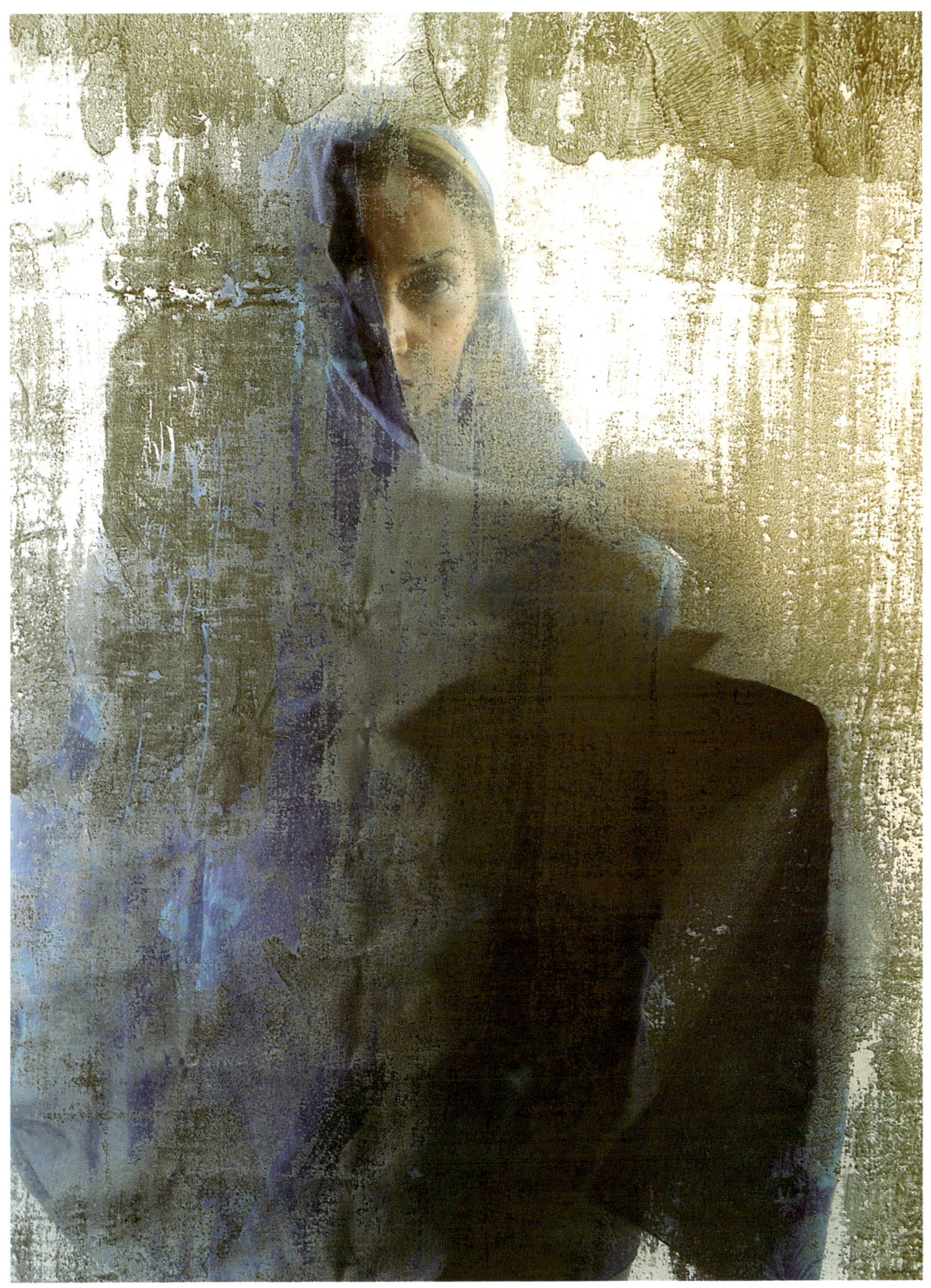

CTRL+ALT+DEL SERIES

2006-07

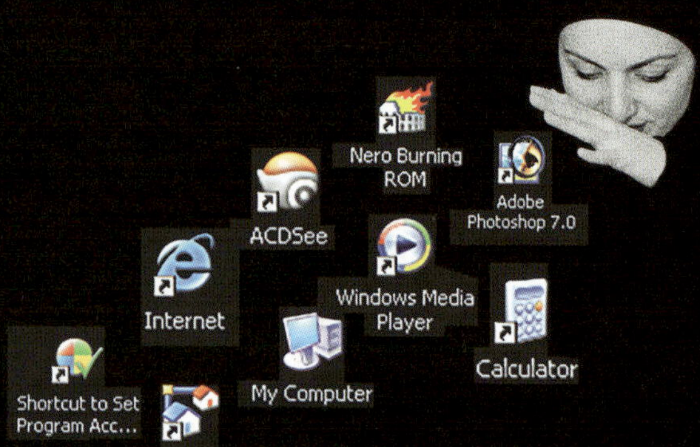

Nero Burning ROM
Adobe Photoshop 7.0
ACDSee
Internet
Windows Media Player
Shortcut to Set Program Acc...
My Computer
Calculator
Nero

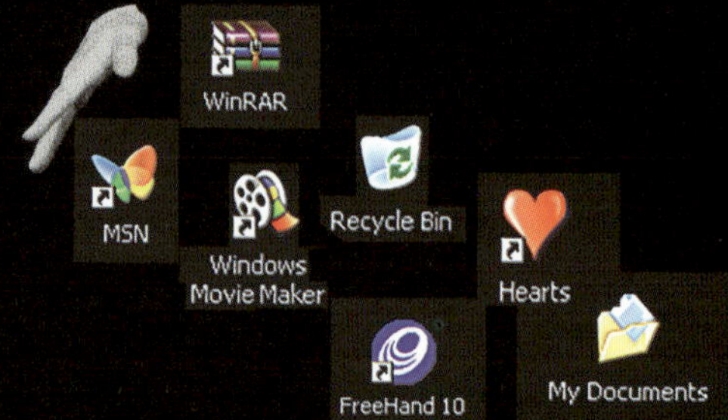

WinRAR
MSN
Windows Movie Maker
Recycle Bin
Hearts
FreeHand 10
My Documents

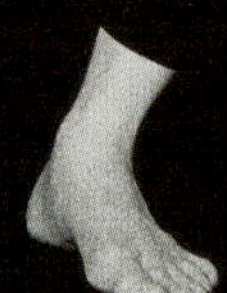

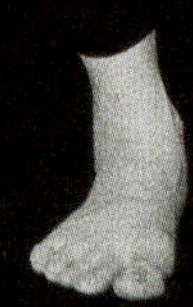

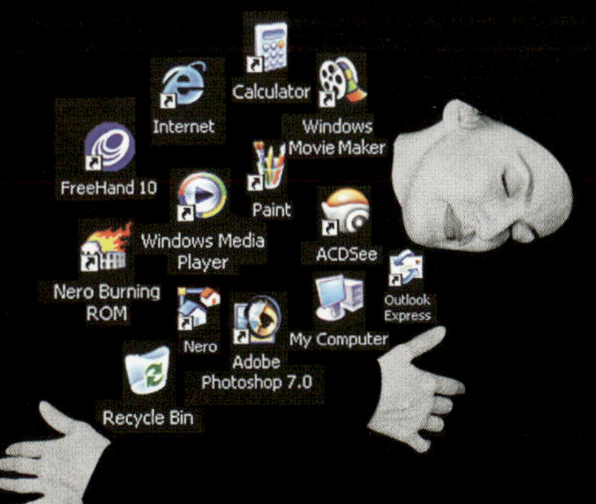
Internet
Calculator
Windows
Movie Maker
FreeHand 10
Paint
Windows Media
Player
ACDSee
Nero Burning
ROM
Nero
My Computer
Outlook
Express
Adobe
Photoshop 7.0
Recycle Bin
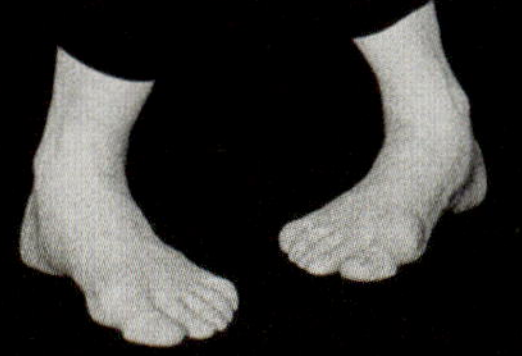

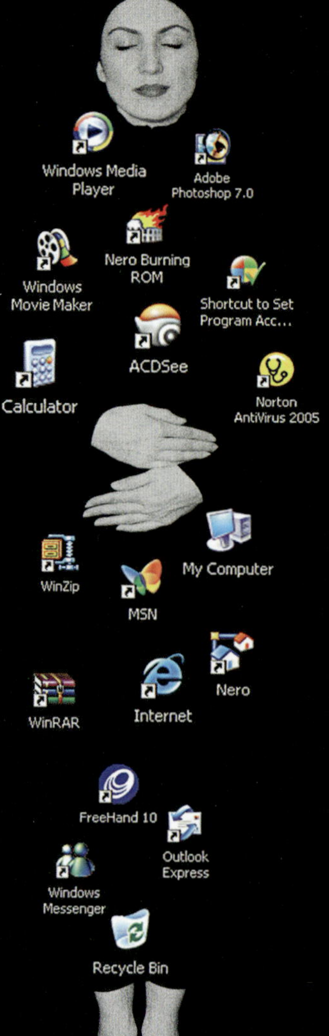

Windows Media Player
Adobe Photoshop 7.0
Nero Burning ROM
Windows Movie Maker
Shortcut to Set Program Acc...
Calculator
ACDSee
Norton AntiVirus 2005
WinZip
My Computer
MSN
WinRAR
Internet
Nero
FreeHand 10
Outlook Express
Windows Messenger
Recycle Bin

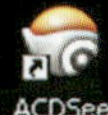
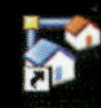
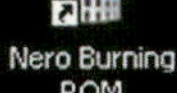
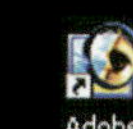
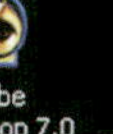
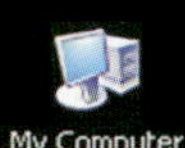
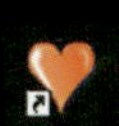
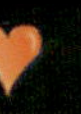
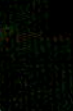
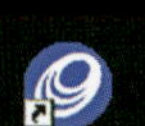
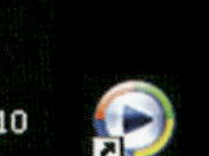
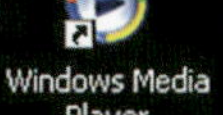
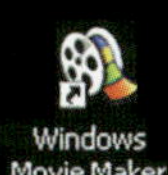
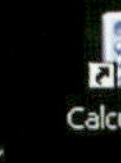
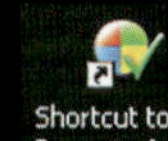
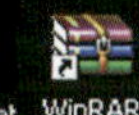
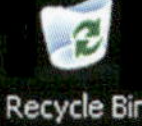
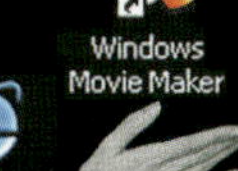
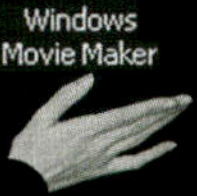
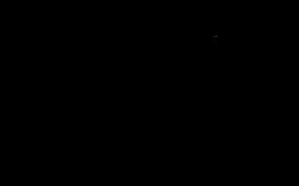
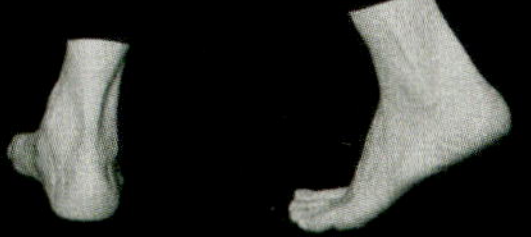

ACDSee
Nero
Nero Burning ROM
Adobe Photoshop 7.0
My Computer
Hearts
FreeHand 10
Windows Media Player
MSN
Internet
Windows Movie Maker
Calculator
Shortcut to Set Program Acc...
WinRAR
Recycle Bin

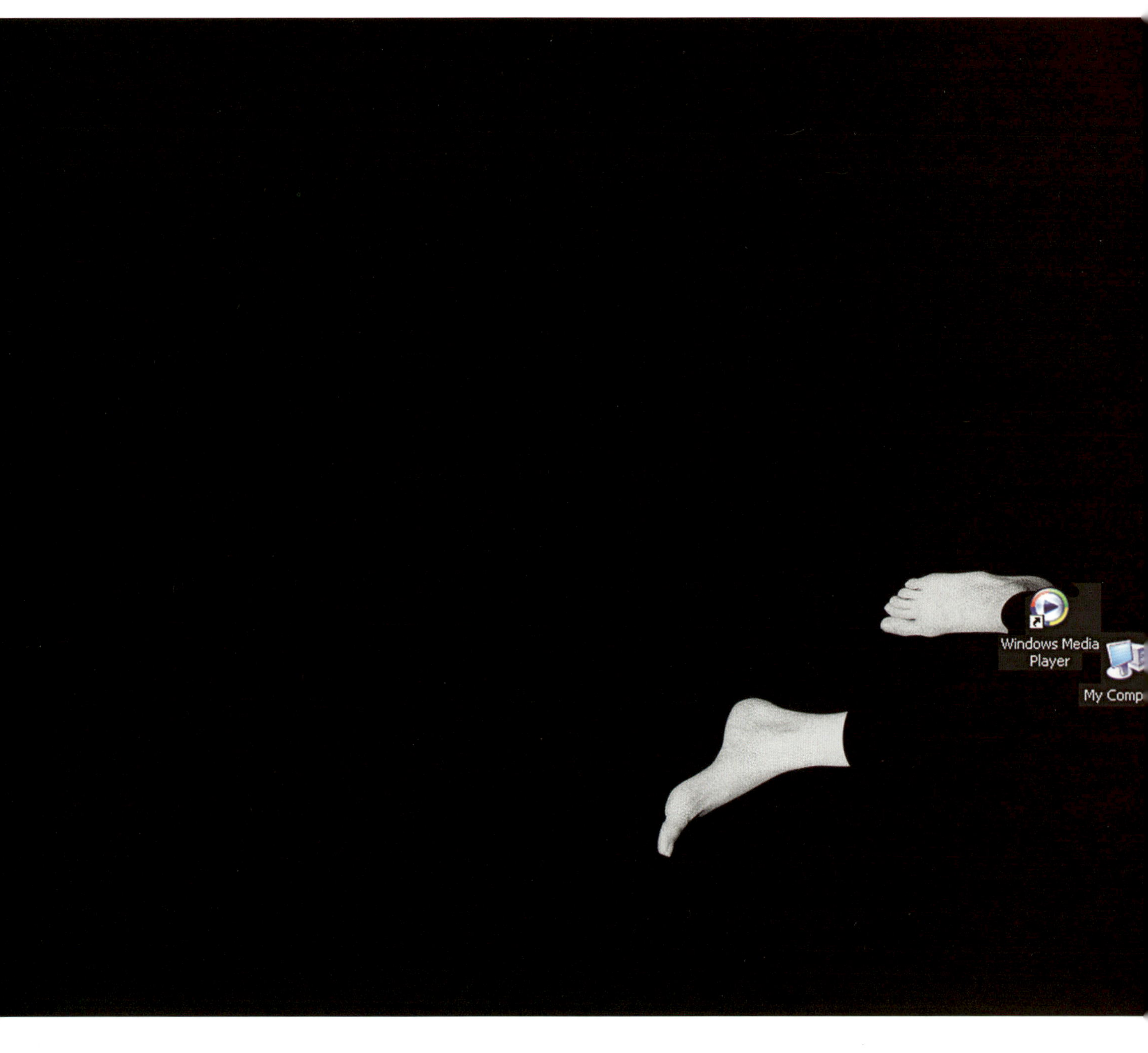

Windows Media Player
My Comp

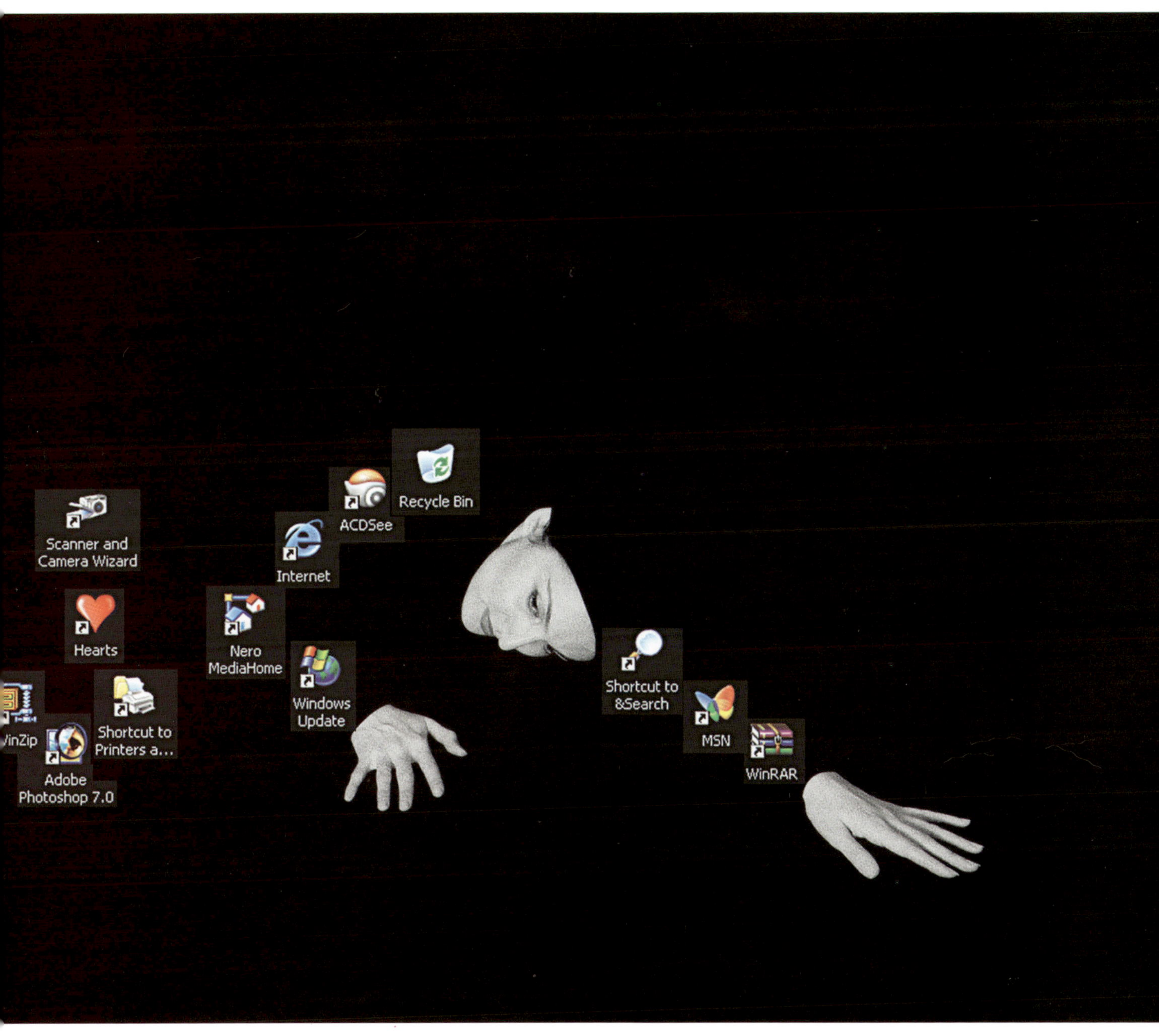

Scanner and Camera Wizard
Hearts
WinZip
Shortcut to Printers a...
Adobe Photoshop 7.0
Nero MediaHome
Internet
ACDSee
Windows Update
Recycle Bin
Shortcut to &Search
MSN
WinRAR

BIOGRAPHY

Shadi Ghadirian was born in 1974 in Tehran, Iran
and graduated with a BA in Photography from the
Azad University, Tehran in 1998.

SELECTED SOLO EXHIBITIONS

2008
Los Angeles County Museum of Art, California

2007
Photography Festival of Istanbul, Turkey
Gallery B21, Dubai

2006
Al Maamal Foundation, East Jerusalem, Palestine

2002
Villa Moda, Kuwait
Silk Road Gallery, Tehran

1999
Golestan Gallery, Tehran

SELECTED GROUP EXHIBITIONS

2008
Word Into Art, DIFC, Dubai

2007
Noorderlicht Photofestival, Netherlands
La Paz, Bolivia
San Diego Convention Centre, California
Silk Road Gallery, Tehran

2006
Inaugura en Tucumán,
Mexico Selyemes Fenyek, Budapest
Le Rectangle, Lyon, France
Representation and Use of the Body in Art,
Galerie Helene Lamarque, Paris
Ey! Iran: Contemporary Iranian Photography,
Gold Coast City Art Gallery, Australia
Images of the Middle East, DCCD,
Copenhagen, Denmark
Word into Art: Artists of the Modern Middle East,
The British Museum, London

The Veiled Mirror,
Contemporary Iranian Photography,
De Santos Gallery, Houston, Texas
French Cultural Centre, Damascus, Syria
Distinctive, Artspace Witzenhausen, Amsterdam
Blessed are the Merciful,
Feigen Contemporary, New York

2005
Third Line Gallery, Dubai
Baudoin Lebon Gallery, Paris
Aeroplastics, Belgium
After the Revolution, San Sebastian, Spain
Rebel Mind Gallery, Berlin
West by East, CCCB, Barcelona

2004
Far Near Distance,
The House of World Cultures (HKW), Berlin
Chobi Mella 3, Bangladesh
Photography Biennale, Luxemburg
Photography Biennale, Moscow
San Jose Museum of Art, California

2003
Ville De Boulogne-Billancourt, France
Sorbonne University, Paris
Konstmuseum, Gothenberg, Sweden
Sharjah International Biennial 6
The Veil, touring exhibition, The New Art Gallery,
Walsall, Liverpool, and Oxford
Harem Fantasies and the New Sheherezades,
touring exhibition, CCCB Barcelona and Lyon

2002
Glimpses of Iran,
Thessaloniki Museum of Photography, Greece
The Museum of Contemporary Art, Tehran

2001
Iranian Contemporary Art,
Barbican Art Centre, London
Regards Persans, Espace Electra, Paris
Fnac, Paris
Space Gallery, Toronto
Photospania Festival, Madrid

2000

Inheritance, Leighton House Museum, London
The House of World Cultures (HKW), Berlin
Ballymena Arts Festival, Northern Ireland
Ekbatana?,
Nikolaj Contemporary Art Centre, Copenhagen
Barg Gallery, Tehran
The Iranian Women's Studies Foundation, Worth
Ryder Gallery at University of California, Berkeley

1998

Sooreh International Photo Exhibition, Tehran
Barg Gallery, Tehran

1997

Group Photo Exhibition (about children),
Aria Gallery, Tehran
*Tehran International Documentary Photo
Exhibition*, Tehran

PUBLIC COLLECTIONS

The British Museum, London

Musée des Arts Contemporains, Centre
Georges Pompidou, Paris

MUMOK (Museum Moderner Kunst Stiftung
Ludwig), Vienna

Los Angeles County Museum of Art, California

The Sackler Gallery, Smithsonian Institution,
Washington DC

Victoria and Albert Museum, London

SELECTED PUBLICATIONS

Iranian Photography Now, edited by Rose Issa
(Hatje Cantz, 2008)

*Thirty Years of Solitude: A Selection of Iranian
Contemporary Films and Photographs by Women*,
by Faryar Javaherian (New Hall, Cambridge, 2007)

Word into Art, Artists of the Modern Middle East,
by Venetia Porter (The British Museum Press,
London, 2006 and 2008)

'Iran: I Awake in Your Eyes' in *Private*, vol. 30
(Oriano Sportelli, Ravenna, Summer 2005)

Occident Vist des d'Orient, by Abdelwahab Meddeb
(CCCB, Barcelona, 2005)

Entfernte Nähe: Neue Positionen Iranischer Künstler
(Far Near Distance: Contemporary Positions of Iranian
Artists), edited by Shaheen Merali & Martin Hager
(Haus der Kulturen der Welt, Berlin, 2004)

Veil: Veiling, Representation and Contemporary Art,
edited by David A. Bailey & Gilane Tawadros (Oxford
Museum of Modern Art, Iniva, London, 2003–4)

Haft: sept artistes contemporains iraniens, by Farhad
Khosrokhavar & Michket Krifa (Somogy Editions
d'Art, Ville de Boulogne-Billancourt, 2003)

Harem Fantasies and the New Sheherezades,
(CCCB, Barcelona, Spain, 2003)

Regards Persans: Iran, une révolution photographique,
by Michket Krifa (Éditions des Musées de la Ville
de Paris, Paris, 2001)

Iranian Contemporary Art, by Rose Issa
(Booth-Clibborn Editions, London, 2001)

Ekbatana? by Elisabeth Delin Hansen (Nikolaj
Contemporary Art Centre, Copenhagen, 2000)

TANK Arabica, Tank Magazine (London, 1999)

'I must say something
I must say something
In the shivering moment at daybreak
When space blends with something strange
Like the portents of puberty
I want
To surrender to some revolt
I want
To pour down out of that vast cloud
I want
To say no no no'
Forugh Farrokhzad
Another Birth